Personal Finance for Teens

D0168278

Carol H. Cox

ISBN-13: 978-1-5234-0416-2

Disclaimer

This book is for general educational purposes. The author has not considered the specific financial circumstances of any individuals and has not engaged in providing any form of professional advice. This document is not a substitute for qualified professionals. If individuals require financial, legal, or other expert advice, the services of a competent professional person should be sought.

The author has no liability or responsibility to any person or entity with respect to any loss or damage caused, or alleged to have been caused, directly or indirectly, by the information contained in this book.

ii

For my parents

Contents

Introduction

I f you've picked up this book, it's probably because you're wondering what you need to know about money management before leaving home. Soon you may find yourself transitioning from living with your family to life on your own away at college or to working fulltime and living in an apartment. This is a great time to get a handle on your personal finances, before your life gets more complicated.

Most high schools don't require students to take a course in personal finance. The Internet provides lots of material on money management, but searching through this digital thicket of information can be frustratingly time consuming, and the data is not always relevant for teens, complete, or correct. Parents can be wonderful resources, but sometimes they don't have the time or knowledge to cover all of the important personal finance topics with their teens.

This is why I wrote *Personal Finance for Teens*. It's written to provide high school students, like you, with easy access to crucial money management information. This book gives an overview of key financial concepts and the actions that you can take now to make the most of what you have. The information is presented simply and logically, with financial terms explained throughout the book and again at the end in the extensive glossary.

Having a master's degree in business has helped me successfully coach my daughters on financial matters as they have transitioned from high school to college. My concern is for those of you who don't have this kind of help. *Personal Finance for Teens* is my way of offering assistance. Read it, try out some of the suggestions, discuss it with family members if you like, and follow up with some of the resources mentioned at the end of each chapter.

Personal Finance for Teens is filled with vital information on topics such as the following:

- Effective job-search skills.

- How to budget your money and where to keep it.

- How income taxes affect your paycheck.

- The importance of credit scoring.

- College financial aid basics.

- How to begin saving early for retirement.

At the close of each chapter, listed under "Additional Resources," are helpful references for gaining a broader and deeper understanding of the chapter topics.

This book is a great place to begin your personal finance education. This material will allow you to become more familiar and comfortable with financial terms you'll come across increasingly in daily life. Your interactions with banks, credit companies, employers, and investment companies will be easier once you understand what these institutions offer and how they can help you.

I've made *Personal Finance for Teens* relatively short and to the point so that you can quickly get the essential facts that you need. The chapters are designed to be read in sequence, some chapters building on earlier ones. But, if you're already familiar with a subject, then feel free to skip ahead. At the end of every chapter is a "Recap" (review) of important areas covered in the chapter for reference.

Here is a summary of each chapter:

Chapter 1. Where to safely keep your money while minimizing the cost to you.

Chapter 2. Job search techniques, resume basics, and interviewing tips.

Chapter 3. An introduction to taxes and withholding.

Chapter 4. How to create a workable spending plan.

Chapter 5. The importance of a good credit history and how to build one.

Chapter 6. An introduction to credit cards and how to best use them.

Chapter 7. Strategies for making the cost of college more manageable.

Chapter 8. Cost factors, not just the purchase price, to consider when buying a car.

Chapter 9. How to use your age to your advantage when saving for retirement.

Personal financial planning is a lifelong process. Hopefully, after reading this book, you will be inspired to learn more. Money worries can become one of the top stresses in your life. Your financial situation can greatly impact your relationships, where you live and work, and even your health. In short, the quality of your finances can affect the quality of your life. When it comes to buying a car, renting an apartment, getting a job, obtaining insurance, and in many other instances, having your finances in good shape can make things go much more smoothly.

If you want to learn how to manage and improve your financial life then read on...

Carol H. Cox

[I welcome your feedback! If you have any comments, or suggestions about this book or other topics, you can reach me at CarolHCoxAuthor@gmail.com or follow me on Twitter @CarolHCoxAuthor. Thank you!]

Note: Internet References

Because Internet web addresses change frequently and some of them are quite long, I have sometimes substituted an Internet search reference for the exact link.

An example search reference looks something like the following:

Internet search>> *site: studentaid.ed.gov scholarships and grants*

If you type what is shown in italics, after the words "Internet search>>," into a search engine (like Google or Bing), you will receive links having "studentaid.ed.gov" in the address (a U.S. Department of Education website). These links should lead to information about "scholarships and grants" on that website.

Click on the top search results after skipping any advertising links to get to the appropriate webpages.

1

Managing a Checking Account

H ave you ever walked into a school club meeting, or some other social situation, where you knew no one? It can be incredibly awkward and intimidating. Now imagine that you know something about a couple of the people in the room, or maybe you participate in the same sport or have mutual friends. You have a thread of conversation material to start with. It's not quite so uncomfortable anymore.

Well, this chapter is designed to familiarize you with the world of banking, and it will hopefully make you a little more at ease when dealing with financial institutions. Now is an excellent time to get acquainted with them.

If you don't already have a checking account, you'll probably need one soon. The checking account is a basic, flexible, and convenient financial account that banking institutions offer consumers and businesses for storing money. These financial institutions provide a secure place for customers to deposit money, and they supply customers with guaranteed ready access to their deposits. Money is typically available by check writing, using teller machines, visiting bank branches, accessing mobile apps, and other means.

In exchange, banking institutions can loan out some of the deposited funds and earn money by charging borrowers for the use of this money. Not to worry, banking institutions are heavily regulated and insured to keep your money safe—there are federal rules limiting the amount of customer deposits that can be lent out.

Checking Account Features

A checking account is a very liquid account (it's easy to withdraw your money). You virtually have access to your funds whenever you need them, and, as an added layer of security, most money in these accounts is insured by the federal government. In this age of *automated teller machines* (ATMs), online bill paying and mobile banking, a checking account can be extremely useful, and if you choose the right type of account and manage it well, it won't cost you much, if anything, to do so.

You may already have a savings account. Perhaps you have some money stashed in such an account, from birthdays, allowances, and odd jobs. That's great for long-term savings, but as you become more financially sophisticated you can benefit from the flexibility of a checking account.

Savings accounts weren't designed for customers to use as a frequent bill-paying vehicle. The Federal Reserve (the Fed) has rules that limit the frequency of certain types of savings account transactions. In addition, savings accounts virtually never have check-writing privileges. On the other hand, savings accounts are great for building up money. You can make an unlimited number of deposits to them.

With a checking account, withdrawals can be made by check, by using a debit card to make purchases, or by using online or mobile tools to transfer funds or pay bills. Withdrawals can be made as frequently as you choose. You can make deposits into your checking account by using an ATM, going to a branch office, or having money electronically sent to your account, such as with *direct deposit* of your paycheck.

Direct Deposit

If you have a job where you receive a regular paycheck, you will likely be given the opportunity to sign up for direct deposit. Direct deposit allows your employer to electronically deposit your salary directly into your bank account without having to physically issue you a paper check.

It gives you quicker availability to your money, without having to deposit your paycheck or worry about losing it. Employers like it because it saves them the cost of issuing checks.

Another plus, banks that normally charge a monthly checking account maintenance fee will often waive the fee if you direct deposit a minimum monthly amount into your account.

Checking accounts are offered by financial institutions such as commercial banks or *credit unions*. Most banks and credit unions have information-rich websites where you can view online account statements, monitor your account activity, use online bill paying, and can set up email alerts for such things as flagging a low account balance or for notifying you when a deposit is received into your account.

Many institutions also offer mobile banking apps for account access with a smartphone or tablet. These mobile apps allow you to do things like check your account balance, pay bills, transfer money, locate ATM/banking centers, and even deposit a check on the fly by snapping a picture of it and transmitting the photo.

Nearly all checking accounts are insured by either the Federal Depository Insurance Corporation (FDIC) or the National Credit Union Administration (NCUA). Money is insured for up to $250,000 per depositor per bank or credit union. If your bank or credit union were to run into some financial problems, your money up to the insurance limit would still be there for you. (To check if your bank or credit union has insurance coverage, go to either *www.fdic.gov* or *www.mycreditunion.gov*.)

Credit Unions

Credit unions (CUs) are not-for-profit financial institutions organized and run for the benefit of the members (the depositors). Typically, membership is organized around a specific group, such as people of a particular geographic region, employees of the same organization, or alumni association members. CUs focus on community savings and community lending activities. They provide many of the same services as banks, like savings and checking accounts, credit cards, and online banking services.

CUs are known for their personal service and community focus, as well as low fees. The majority of CUs belong to ATM shared networks, providing thousands of locations at which to do business. CU accounts are insured up to $250,000 per depositor per credit union by the National Credit Union Administration (NCUA).

Federal Reserve (the Fed)

The Federal Reserve is the central bank of the United States. The Fed seeks to maintain a healthy and stable U.S. economy, keep unemployment rates low, keep inflation under control, monitor and regulate banking institutions, and protect consumer credit rights.

Selecting a Bank and Checking Account

One of the easiest places to begin your search may be with a bank or credit union where you or your family already have an account. They may offer a "student" or "teen" checking account. Many banking institutions provide these type of low-cost accounts.

If your family doesn't have a relationship with a bank or credit union, then you can do an Internet search for "teen or student checking accounts." There is also a list of helpful websites at the end of this chapter under "Additional Resources."

Teen checking accounts are desirable because they are designed to be easy to open and inexpensive to maintain. Look for these features when selecting a checking account:

Things You Want in a Checking Account

✓ A small initial deposit to open an account, $50 or less

✓ No maintenance fees

✓ No, or a very low, minimum balance requirement

✓ Free ATM usage within the banking or credit union network

✓ Bank or credit union network ATMs near where you expect to be living, or a good ATM *fee-reimbursement* program if you use ATMs outside of the network

✓ Easy online and mobile access with up-to-date information

Don't hesitate to ask plenty of questions—these companies want your business, and they are hoping that you will become a loyal customer, depositing lots of money over the years and using many of their banking services.

ATM/Debit Cards

An ATM/debit card is two cards in one linked to your checking account. As an ATM card it allows you to get cash directly from your account via an ATM—you put your card in the machine, enter your *personal identification number* (PIN), and withdraw money from the machine.

As a debit card it accesses the money in your checking account when you use your card to pay for something. The money is automatically deducted from your checking account. When you use an ATM/debit card to either get cash or pay for something, you are using your own money, not borrowing money.

These cards are often just referred to as ATM cards.

If you are under age 18 and want a checking account with an ATM card, you will likely have to open a joint account with a parent or guardian as co-signer on the account (note: for simplicity, this book will use the word "parent," from now on to also mean guardian).

Being able to monitor your checking account online or by using mobile banking apps are important features. They can help you manage your spending, keep your account balance above any required minimum, and avoid being *overdrawn* in your account (spending more money than you actually have on deposit).

ATM availability is also an important consideration in your choice, especially if you plan to make frequent withdrawals and deposits to your account. Think of where you plan to be living for the next few years. If the bank or credit union you are considering has a very small ATM network in your chosen city, then you might end up using out-of-network ATMs to get cash, meaning ATMs belonging to other companies. And if you do so, you may be charged a fee by your own bank or credit union, something like $3 per usage, and also a fee by the organization that owns the ATM you use. In total, this could end up costing you around $6 or more per transaction. If you use out-of-network ATMs frequently, these charges can add up quickly. (Of course, if your bank or credit union has a generous ATM fee-reimbursement program, you'll get some or all of these fees back.)

Bigger well-known banks tend to have large ATM networks. However, smaller banks and credit unions have figured out how to consolidate into large co-op networks. These smaller financial institutions share usage of each other's ATMs free of charge. For example, many credit unions belong to a co-op network that has nearly 30,000 ATMs nationwide and has thousands of "shared" branches where any of the network credit union members can conduct banking business. (Go to *www.mycreditunion.gov* to find out more about credit unions and locations near you.)

19

ATM Fee Reimbursement

Some banks and credit unions offer partial or total refunds of fees that a customer incurs when using an ATM outside of the bank's or credit union's network. The bank or credit union adds back money to the customer's account to reimburse the customer for ATM-usage fees up to a given monthly limit.

Opening an Account

As mentioned earlier, banking institutions have age restrictions for opening checking accounts. If you are under age 18, you will likely need to bring your parent with you to be a co-signer on the account (at some banks and credit unions the parent is also required to have a separate account in addition to the co-signed account at the financial institution).

You can explain to your parent that you want to become more financially independent and knowledgeable, to learn how banking works, and that you need a co-signer to open up a checking account. More than likely they will be happy to help.

When your parent is on board with your plans, find an hour when you are both free to go to the bank or credit union to open an account. Check ahead of time to find out what identifications are needed. Usually, you will need to bring one or two IDs, like a driver's license, birth certificate, social security card, or passport.

At the meeting, the financial officer may ask you to choose a PIN (personal identification number), of four or more digits, for your ATM card—you might want to have one in mind before arriving. (Of course, stay clear of numbers like your birth date or social security number, since these numbers have security issues.)

Institutions usually require an initial deposit for a new account. Student accounts typically have a low initial deposit minimum, perhaps $50 or so. The exact amount varies by bank or credit union. You can find out ahead of time how much money to bring to the meeting.

When you and your parent sit down with the bank or credit union officer, ask the officer to explain the major features and the fees of the checking account. Don't hesitate to ask a lot of questions. Consider asking the following ones:

Questions about Fees and Services

- Is there a fee if my balance falls below a certain level and how much?

- Can I use my bank's or credit union's ATMs an unlimited number of times for free each month?

- Will I be charged for using my ATM card at other non-network ATMs and how much?

- Do you reimburse ATM fee charges? How many and how much?

- What online banking services are there?

- What happens if I *overdraft* my account (spend more than is in the account)?

- What kind of overdraft protection services are there and what are the fees?

- What kind of identity theft protection is there and what is the customer's financial responsibility?

At the account setup, you may be given a small number of starter checks and a *transaction register* (also called a check register) for keeping track of your account activity. The register is a slim check-sized booklet that you can carry with you to record your daily transactions (see Figure 1.1 later in this chapter). You may also be issued a temporary ATM card while your permanent one, which will be mailed to you later, is being created.

Bank Accounts for Non-U.S. Citizens

You do not need to be a U.S. citizen to open a bank account, but you will be required to provide proof of who you are (such as your name, address, date of birth, official identification cards, and government documents). Each bank has its own policies designed to comply with federal requirements, so check with the specific financial institution where you are interested in opening an account.

Minimizing Account Fees

If you've taken a commercial flight recently, you may have noticed the variety of fees that can be added to the price of a ticket. There can be extra charges for checked bags, food service, headphones, pillows, blankets, and so on.

Banks have a similar model. There can be fees for such actions as transferring funds, using another organization's ATMs, carrying a balance below the minimum, and having monthly statements mailed to you. These fees can shrink your checking account balance in no time.

When you open an account, the bank or credit union officer will likely tell you about some of these fees and supply you with literature about their costs. You may forget many of the details the minute you walk out of the lobby doors, but if you make the mistake of ignoring these fees, like many people do, you may eventually find that you've wasted hundreds of dollars over the years on such extra charges.

Most of these costs can be avoided with a little forward planning. Here is a list of things you can do to keep fees to a minimum:

Reducing Fees

1. Know your bank's or credit union's ATM locations and use only those to avoid non-network ATM fees.

2. Minimize any ATM usage fees by making larger less frequent withdrawals.

3. Review your balance daily to avoid overdrawing your account.

4. If you have a savings account with the same banking institution as your checking account, have the accounts linked to automatically transfer money from savings to checking if you overdraw your account (transfer fees are generally lower than overdraft fees).

5. Use your ATM card to get cash back when you make purchases at retailers, they typically don't charge a fee (for example, grocery and drug stores).

6. If you see an unexpected fee on your monthly account statement, call or chat online with your bank or credit union customer service representative and ask them to

waive the fee—they often will if it is the first time that it has happened.

7. Set up email and text alerts to notify you if your account balance falls below a certain amount or when deposits and deductions have been made to your account.

8. Agree to receive all of your account information online to avoid charges for printed and mailed statements.

9. Balance your checking account monthly (see "Keeping an Eye on Your Checking Account" later in this chapter), and investigate any fees to figure out why they occurred so that you can avoid them in the future.

Overdraft Protection

We all make mistakes. You may one day accidently overdraw your account, essentially trying to complete a checking account transaction for more money than you have on deposit. Maybe you forgot to write down a big withdrawal you made a few days ago, or some emergency occurred where you drained your checking account. When your bank or credit union extends you overdraft protection, your underfunded transaction is allowed to go through.

Where does the extra money come from? Your bank or credit union may use its own funds or money that you have in another account at the same institution to cover the difference between the actual amount that exists in your checking account and the amount of money that the transaction requires.

For example, if you make out a $100 check to a friend, but you forgot that you paid your cell phone bill yesterday and that you now only have $90 in your checking account, then with overdraft protection your bank covers your account for the remaining $10 when your friend cashes the check. Of course, your bank will require you to pay back the $10, which they've, basically loaned you, and will charge you a fee in addition— perhaps $35 or more.

Usually a less expensive way of covering any overdrafts is to link a checking account with a savings account that you have at the same institution. This will allow for the automatic transfer of money from savings to checking account if you have a cash shortage (this assumes you have enough money in your savings account to cover things). A transfer fee may apply, something like $12 or so.

It's important to realize that each time you overdraw your account, even if it's in the same day, fees may be charged. If you overdraw your account three separate times in one day, you may have to pay three sets of fees, and financial institutions may also add an extended overdraft fee if you have not repaid the bank or credit union within a certain number of days. This can get expensive, quickly.

Overdraft protection can be extended not only to check transactions but also to ATM withdrawals, purchases you make with your ATM card, and automatic online bill pay. (Some types of overdraft coverage require your permission—see the "New Overdraft Protection Rules" textbox.)

If you find you're using overdraft protection repeatedly, take this as a sign that you need to make some changes in your financial life. The best policy is not to spend more money than you have, then you won't be bothered with any of these charges. Keeping track of your bank balance is important.

> ### New Overdraft Protection Rules
>
> As of July 2010, the Fed instituted new rules to better protect consumers against growing bank fees.
>
> In the past, some financial institutions would automatically apply overdraft protection to a customer's checking account. Now banks and credit unions need consumer consent for particular overdraft services, such as overdraft on ATM and one-time debit card transactions.
>
> Financial institutions can still automatically apply overdraft protection for check writing and automatic payments. However, if the bank policies allow for it, consumers can request that overdraft protection not be applied in these situations. Check with your bank for the current rules.

Internet Banks

These days, people have another alternative to traditional brick-and-mortar banks: Internet banks. There are several Internet banks, such as EverBank and Ally Bank, that offer online savings and checking accounts. They are real banks with deposits insured by the FDIC, there just isn't any physical bank with tellers and bank officers that customers can visit—business is handled via computer, telephone, or mail. Higher *interest* rates paid on deposits and lower account minimums and fees make online bank accounts attractive.

Interest

When money is borrowed, the borrower usually pays the lender interest, compensation for having the use of this money. It is usually stated as a percentage of the amount of money borrowed.

A customer who deposits money into an online bank account is letting the bank use that money until the customer withdraws it. The bank pays the customer interest for "borrowing" the money.

The absence of branch offices staffed with employees, can result in much lower overhead costs for online banks, which means that online banks can pass on some of these savings to customers in the form of higher interest rates paid on customer deposits, particularly savings accounts. Online bank checking accounts frequently have very low, or no, minimum balance requirements, no maintenance fees, offer check-writing privileges, accept automatic deposit, and offer ATM cards. Many online banks belong to large shared-ATM networks and some have ATM fee reimbursement plans.

Maintaining an online savings account for money that you don't need to tap regularly, such as accumulated savings for an expensive item like a car, may be one of the best uses of online banks. Online savings accounts generally offer much higher interest rates than do online checking accounts.

An Internet bank account can be a good addition to or an alternative to a traditional bank account, particularly when used for long-term savings.

Keeping an Eye on Your Checking Account

What's the point of carefully reviewing your monthly checking account statements—it's history, right?

First of all, financial institutions aren't perfect. Sometimes they make record keeping errors, or you may disagree with a fee you have been charged. The sooner you flag the issue the easier it is to fix. Second, you can spot unusual activity, such as fraud (identity theft), and take care of it immediately. And, last of all, looking at your monthly statement will give you a valuable snapshot of all your banking activities for the month, great information for following a spending plan.

Ideally, after you complete an ATM transaction or make a purchase with your card or write a check, you will record this activity in your transaction register. (If you don't have a register your bank or credit union can usually supply you with one.)

The following figure shows a completed page from an example transaction register. The far right column of the register is labeled "balance." Here you can keep a running total of how much money is in your checking account as you withdraw money, write checks, make purchases, and deposit funds.

Keeping an accurate running balance can help you avoid accidently overdrawing your account, which can lead to unnecessary fees. It's best to record financial activity right away and to keep a copy of receipts until you've reviewed your monthly statement. Memories can fade quickly, and having a record of what you did will make reviewing your monthly statement much easier if you want to research something that looks incorrect.

Example Transaction Register

Check Number	Date	Transaction Description	Payment, Withdrawal or Fee	Deposit	Balance
					565.67
	1/12/15	ATM cash (pizza)	20.00		545.67
	1/15	Deposit (paycheck)		125.00	670.67
	1/16	Transfer to savings account	50.00		620.67
#302	1/20	Galt Senior High (fieldtrip)	65.00		555.67
	1/21	Starbuck's (debit card used)	3.60		552.07
	1/25	Deposit (paycheck)		125.00	677.07
	2/07	Transfer to savings account	50.00		627.07
#303	2/10	Sarah Johnson (concert tickets)	48.50		578.57

FIGURE 1.1

Example Monthly Bank Statement First Page

Pacific Bank – Checking Account		
Angela Smith		Page 1 of 4
222 Oak Ave		1/10/15 to 2/09/15
Grove, CA 92222		
Account Number	1111-2222-3333	
Beginning Balance as of 1/10/15	$565.67	
Deposits and Other Additions	$250.00	
ATM and Debit Card Subtractions	$23.60	
Other Subtractions	$165.00	
Ending Balance as of 2/09/15	$627.07	

FIGURE 1.2 Statement corresponds to Figure 1.1 transaction register.

The first page of an example bank statement in Figure 1.2 corresponds to the transaction register in Figure 1.1. Every month, your bank will generate a monthly checking account statement. It will detail, by date and dollar amount, what transactions occurred in your account for the month, including checks processed, deposits received, ATM withdrawals, debit card purchases, and banking fees.

The statement can be compared (reconciled) with the register for the same time period. When reconciling the two documents, it's important to note the date of each transaction in the register as compared with the ending date of the bank statement. For instance, in the preceding examples the ending balance on the register ($578.57) is smaller than the ending balance on the bank statement ($627.07). This is because check #303, written for Sarah Johnson for $48.50, was written on 2/10/15, after the bank statement closing date of 2/09/15, so that check hadn't cleared (been processed) in time to be included in the bank statement. This explains the difference between the two balances.

Whether you receive a printed statement in the mail or access one online, either can be used for your monthly statement review. This process of reconciling your transaction record with your monthly statement is called "balancing your checking account." To stay on top of your account, it's important to do this monthly review.

Following is a list of review steps:

Monthly Checking Account Statement Review

1. Compare the closing balance (ending balance) from your checking account statement with the running balance from your transaction register that is closest in time to the account statement closing date. (In the preceding examples, the statement closing balance date was 2/09/15 and the nearest transaction register date was 2/10/15.)

2. Are the two balances the same? If not, see if there are any entries in the register that are not listed in the account statement. Using a calculator, adjust the statement balance for these not-yet-recorded entries, and see if the adjusted statement balance now equals the register balance. If so, the two balance reconcile and you're done.

31

3. If the adjusted statement balance still doesn't equal the register balance, then look for entries on your statement that aren't reflected in your register. If they look correct, add these forgotten transactions into your register to get an adjusted register balance. Now compare the adjusted register balance with the adjusted statement balance. If the missing entries are correct and they explain the difference between your register and statement, then you've reconciled your account and you're done.

4. If something is still off, something on your statement that is not in your transaction register and doesn't look correct, then go through your ATM receipts and paid bills to see if you forgot some transactions. If it still looks wrong, then contact your bank to investigate.

5. Review any banking fees or service charges listed on your statement, and find out why they happened and how you can change your habits to avoid them in the future.

6. If there are no bank errors and all the transactions are listed, and your statement and register still don't square, then you've probably made a math error in your totals or transposed a number on your register.

7. To find the error, review your register entries, line by line, and check your math. (If the difference is small, it may not be worth taking the time to do this—just make a correcting entry in your register to fix the balance.)

Repeat these steps every month when you get a new statement. Reviewing your checking account statement regularly will help you to better track your spending, lessen bank fees, and catch identity theft.

Recap: Checking Accounts

1. Discuss your checking account needs with your parents and see if they will co-sign if needed. (A checking account with a linked ATM card usually requires an adult co-signer if you are under age 18.)

2. Check with your family's existing bank or credit union for "student" or "teen checking accounts", and search online to find other banks or credit unions that have these types of accounts.

3. Look for banking institutions that have ATMs near where you expect to be living or that have a good ATM fee reimbursement policy.

4. Choose a bank or credit union by comparing fees, account minimums, ATM accessibility, fee reimbursement programs, and online tools.

5. Schedule an appointment to open a checking account (bring necessary IDs and the initial deposit amount).

6. Think up a secure and easy to remember PIN of four or more digits for your ATM card.

7. Review your account online frequently to avoid overdraft fees, catch any identity theft, and maintain your spending targets.

8. Do a monthly checking account statement review to ensure all transactions are accounted for, to catch any errors, to keep fees to a minimum, and to track spending.

Additional Resources

- ✓ These four banks offer student/teen checking accounts:

  Bank of America

  Chase

  US Bank

  Wells Fargo

- ✓ Use this site to find credit unions that may offer student/teen checking accounts:

  www.mycreditunion.gov

- ✓ These two websites are useful for finding banks by geographic region and other criteria:

  www.findabetterbank.com

  www.nerdwallet.com

- ✓ Webpages for some well-known online banks can be found at:

  www.ally.com

  www.capitalone360.com

  www.discoverbank.com

2

Getting a Job

Wouldn't it be nice to have a little more cash in your pocket? Wouldn't it be great to beef up your *resume* for college applications? Do you want to get more firsthand knowledge about your field of interest? Or how about saving some extra money for something special you've been dreaming about? A job may be the answer, whether as a volunteer counselor at a kids' summer camp, or being paid as a "gofer" (go for this, go for that) in an office, or as a cashier at the local grocery store, or having a self-created venture as a tutor.

There are so many different kinds of jobs that it's hard to know where to begin. Answering a few questions about what you want from a job may help. Consider the following questions:

- Are you looking to make some spending money or saving cash for college?

- Is your primary concern getting work experience in a particular field, whether paid or not?

- Are you looking to build certain skills, like computer expertise or youth mentoring?

As an example, let's say that sports medicine is your area of interest and you want to emphasize this on your future college applications. Then you might aim for employment in a summer sports program or a local medical office. If money is not a major worry, look for volunteer positions as well as paid jobs.

Trying to save money to buy a car?—then perhaps a self-created venture is what you need (like using your computer skills as a webpage designer).

If you know your motivation for getting a job, then it's easier to make decisions about where to focus your energies and who to approach for help. And you're more likely to succeed in your search.

Once you've zeroed in on why you are seeking employment, and in what field, then it's time to find individuals who may be able to help you connect with the right people who can provide opportunities.

Network Angels

Even though you may not know someone who actually works in a given field, there's a good chance that you know someone who knows someone else who would be able to help. Frequently, the most effective job search techniques involve networking, tapping into those relationships you have in order to find people who can help. Let's call them *network angels*.

Truthfully, employers often prefer hiring someone who has been introduced or recommended to them by a colleague, friend, or relative whose opinion they value. Person-to-person recommendations are how many jobs are filled.

Some people find networking uncomfortable—they feel like they're using someone to get ahead. But realize that when you're up front with your friend, relative, or acquaintance and tell them what your goal is, there is no slight-of-hand involved—you're not tricking anyone. All of us have had some

36

help along the way. Most people really enjoy helping a young person get ahead in life. Just remember to show your gratitude to others for their assistance by sending a simple email or making a phone call to thank to them.

So who are your network angels?

Opportunities are all around you—perhaps a cousin, the neighbor you dog-sit for, a pastor, a teacher, or even a salesperson where you shop can be a contact point. Anyone of these people may be able to connect you with someone in your area of interest, or a person who knows someone else who can help you. Be bold. You have nothing to lose by asking, but you risk losing a potential job by not asking.

You can communicate with people face-to-face or use social networking tools to help get the word out to friends and family. Here's a networking idea list to ignite your thinking:

Networking Idea List

✓ Relatives—parents, siblings, aunts, uncles, cousins

✓ Other People's Parents—parents of friends

✓ Teachers and Counselors—they have a large network and know a variety of people

✓ Religious Staff—everyone from rabbis and priests, to choir directors, program leaders, and secretaries

✓ Salespersons or Clerks—talk to them at places where you shop

✓ Coaches and Scout Leaders—they love to help youth, that's why they volunteer

✓ Instructors—people who have worked with you and know you

✓ Family Doctors—they are well connected in the community

✓ Family Dentists—they too have a large network

✓ Neighbors—maybe you've done odd jobs for them or they are friends of the family

✓ Other Personal Acquaintances—mail carriers, library workers, pool managers, athletic club personnel, community center workers, and so on

Networking for the Self-Employed

The same relationship mining you do to find a position in an organization also works well for finding self-employment work. Fliers and tear-sheets on bulletin boards and store windows are great, but using word-of-mouth advertising can be just as effective, so use both. Tell everyone you know about your business and the kind of work you do and have fliers and business cards handy. If you have the patience and some computer skills, you can make a webpage to advertise your business.

When you do get a job, the way you handle yourself at work becomes another form of advertising. Go beyond your client's expectations. Do an excellent job, and you will soon be getting referrals, recommendations your client passes on to others, because you do exceptional work. As you do more and more jobs, others will likely pass along word of your quality performance. Before you know it, you may have more work than you can handle!

Research, Research, Research

Okay, let's say that you've gotten contact information or have an opportunity to meet an individual who may have a position available. What's one of the first things you want to do? Research the organization and industry.

Find out as much as you can about the company or group, and the industry in which you would be working. Talk to people who know about the organization. The Internet and libraries have endless amounts of details. Talk to the reference librarian and tell her or him what you're researching. They can be extremely helpful.

Think of your research as the basis for a paper you have to write and that 99 percent of your grade depends on it. Once you have a good understanding of the organization and the field that they operate in, you should be able to ask and answer questions in a way that showcases your acquired knowledge. The fact that you were motivated to find out a lot about your potential employer demonstrates your serious interest in the position. When doing your research, it's helpful to make notes and summaries as you go along, which can later be used to refresh your memory before your first meeting. All of this information you collect will also be very helpful in crafting your resume for the position.

Getting a Resume Together

When you are in job-search mode it's important to have a current resume ready. Job opportunities often appear when you least expect them, and being able to respond quickly could mean the difference between you and someone else getting the position.

While it's recommended to tailor each resume for a specific position, it helps if you've already created a generic resume that you can tweak before giving it to someone. To find material for building a resume look to your past accomplishments.

Resume

It is a concise summarized description of your employment history and qualifications. Resumes typically includes: (1) Your name and contact information; (2) A summary of what type of work you are seeking and what you can bring to a job; (3) Your experience/work history; (4) Your education; (5) Other activities and talents.

As you go through high school, and beginning even as early as middle school, keeping track of your accomplishments can be invaluable information for creating a resume, preparing for a job interview, or even completing college applications. These recorded accomplishments can be in the form of short summaries, where you've written down what you did and what the outcome was. Accomplishments can be anything from character building experiences, to in-depth self-learning, to certifications earned and special classes taken.

It's best to write things down during the experience or soon after, while everything is still fresh in your mind. But even if you're starting from scratch at the end of your high school years, you can still pull these summaries together. You'll probably have to do a little detective work. Some sources of information for building your summaries might be newspaper clippings, old programs and flyers, archived school newsletters, and the memories of family members, teachers and friends.

If this is something that happened a while ago and you can't dig up the exact dates, then estimate the time periods. What's important is that you can note these experiences and discuss how they impacted your life and other people's lives in a positive fashion.

What kind of activities should you document? Well, here's a list of possibilities to give you some idea of what to pay attention to:

Examples of Accomplishments

✓ Co-creating a vegetable garden for your high school

✓ Traveling and singing as a member of your school choir

✓ Tutoring students after school

✓ Volunteering regularly to serve community meals to the homeless

✓ Raising an animal as part of the Future Farmers of America club

✓ Creating and maintaining a website about video gaming

✓ Being a fundraising participant in a 5K/10K charity race

It's helpful to keep these summaries together in one place, perhaps a binder or folder. You can type them up on a computer or write them out by hand. It doesn't matter. What is important is that you create them whenever you've accomplished something noteworthy.

Each summary should include basic information about the what, when, where, who, why, and how nature of the activity. They don't need to be long, half a page should be sufficient. Short and to the point is best. Full sentences aren't necessary—

you're not going to show them to anyone. They're cheat sheets for you to refer to. These quick rundowns of significant accomplishments can be valuable reference tools.

See the following for a list of questions to answer as you complete your summaries:

Accomplishment Summary Questions

1. *What* was the accomplishment?—a one or two sentence description of what you did and any awards or certificates received.

2. *When* and *where* did it happen?—what date(s), where, and how many hours?

3. You and *who* else were involved and who did you help?—who did you collaborate with and who benefited from your actions?

4. *Why* did you decide to take this on?—what was important to you about it?

5. *How* did the experience affect you?—did you improve upon or learn new skills?

6. *How* did you positively impact someone's life?—how did you inspire, teach, or entertain?

Regularly creating these summaries is a good practice to continue throughout your entire working life. Many resume experts recommend keeping an ongoing file about work accomplishments, even when you're not actively looking for other employment. You would include such things as positive or congratulatory emails or memos from your boss or co-workers, employee awards, or favorable performance reviews.

Once you have your accomplishment summaries together you can begin crafting a resume. There are many good books and Internet resources on how to actually structure a resume (some are listed at the end of this chapter). Following are a few helpful guidelines for creating a resume and an example of one resume format (there are many ways to structure one):

Checklist for Building an Effective Resume

✓ Give yourself plenty of time to write a resume, start one now that you can tweak later

✓ Tailor each resume specifically for the position to which you are applying and communicate what skills you can bring to that position.

✓ Be honest—don't put anything in your resume you wouldn't feel comfortable talking about in an interview

✓ Include a professional sounding contact email address (nothing like Froggy337@gmail.com)

✓ Use action verbs (for example, constructed, designed, and initiated) and positive adjectives (for example, self-motivated, precise, and knowledgeable)

✓ Search online for similar job listings to find key words to include in your resume

✓ Always have a savvy English/grammar person proofread your resume

✓ Have a list of positive references ready, people you've already contacted in advance for permission to use their name

Example Resume

Amber Johnson
1111 Prospect Road
My Town, CA 94111
(555) 111-2222
AmberJohnson@website.com

Objective
To work with disadvantaged children, helping them thrive in their educational and cognitive development in a nurturing and stimulating environment.

Education
Western High School
My Town, CA
Future Graduation: June 2016
GPA 3.7

Experience
Girl Scout Camp Counselor, Camp Douglas (July 2014—4 weeks).
--Completed 5-day camp counselor training course.
--Supervised and led a group of six girls in daily arts and crafts, cabin cleanup, recreational activities, and hiking.

Babysitter (2012 to present)
--Weekly 2 hours childcare of eight-year old boy with Down syndrome on Wednesdays after school while the mother runs errands.
--Responsibilities include healthy snack preparation, game playing and social interaction, and tutoring in reading and math.

Sunday School Helper, Methodist Church (2013 to present)
--Assist Sunday school teacher by helping learning-disabled children to complete activities, and by supervising children's outside play, leading sing-alongs, and directing room cleanup.

Certifications/Memberships/Positions
--American Red Cross CPR and First Aid Certification
--Senior Girl Scout (member for 10 years)
--French Club - President, Western High School

Skills and Interests
MS Excel, MS PowerPoint, MS Word, guitar and singing

FIGURE 2.1

44

Cover Letter

Including a cover letter with your resume submission gives you the opportunity to highlight special qualities about yourself, things that make you stand out positively as a great candidate. A cover letter also provides a means for letting a potential employer know about network contacts you have, whether it be a friend, family member, or acquaintance.

First impressions are very important. A cover letter is potentially the very first contact you have with a possible employer, so be sure to address the letter to the right person and spell their name correctly. If you're not sure which person should receive your letter or how to spell their name, try calling the company and speaking with someone in the human resources department, or check the organization's website.

Be creative when it comes to including information about yourself that is relevant to the organization. For example, if you were applying for a summer job working as a salesperson at a retail store, you could highlight that you have customer service experience from helping your Boy Scout troop set up and run garage sale fundraisers. This simple bit of personal information may be just the hook needed to compel someone to continue on and review your resume.

Generally, the letter should be one page. The format varies as to where the names, addresses, and date are positioned at the top of the letter. You can do an Internet search for "cover letter" images to see different styles (see "Additional Resources"). In addition, your school may have a career center where you can look at sample cover letters and resumes.

Following are some basic cover letter guidelines:

Cover Letter Basics

- Top of Letter—the current date and the name of person to whom you're sending the letter, her or his title and business address.

- Salutation—for example, "Dear Ms. Smith."

- Body of Letter—take two or three paragraphs to discuss 1) the specific job you are applying for and how you found out about it (include the name of your contact person, if you have one); and 2) what you can bring to the job that makes you a great candidate—talk a bit about your specific qualities, abilities, or educational background and how they relate to the job.

- Conclusion—this is where you mention the possibility of an interview and close by thanking the person for her or his time.

- Sign-off—with something like "Sincerely," then sign your name (if it's not an email) and type your name below it with your contact information.

- Bottom—let them know your resume is included by typing "Enclosure: Resume" after the sign-off.

After you've spell-checked and grammar-reviewed your cover letter, have someone else look it over. (Your English teacher might be an excellent choice.) Following is Figure 2.2, an example of one possible cover letter format.

Example Cover Letter

May 1, 2015

Dana Smith
Director of Recreation
My Town Department of Parks and Recreation
My Town, CA 94222

Dear Ms. Smith:

The April 23, 2015 article in the *My Town Gazette* entitled "Summer Camps for Disabled Youth" mentioned that your organization is seeking qualified applicants for summer camp counselor positions. I am excited to apply for this position and am confident that I would make a great addition to your counseling staff.

As mentioned in my enclosed resume, last summer I spent a month as a volunteer aid at Camp Douglas, a Girl Scout camp for girls ages 8 to 12. I was responsible for leading and counseling a group of six girls (prior to this I had completed a five-day training course on first aid and leadership). This camp experience was the highlight of my summer.

I have also had the privilege, over the past two years, of regularly babysitting a young boy with Down syndrome, which has been a very rewarding experience. In addition, I frequently work with my church's Sunday school class for kids ages 6 to 11. I have enjoyed this experience of mentoring young children.

I am confident that my many hours as a camp counselor, working with a disabled child, and time spent managing children of varying ages would make me a valuable contributor to your summer counseling staff.

Thank you in advance for your consideration. I look forward to meeting you and interviewing for the camp counselor position.

Sincerely,

Amber Johnson
1111 Prospect Road
My Town, CA 94111
(555) 111-2222
AmberJohnson@website.com

Enclosure: Resume

FIGURE 2.2

Sending a well written cover letter and resume will greatly improve your chances of getting a job. Below are some tips for email submissions:

Tips for Emailing Resumes and Cover Letters

Subject Line – make it helpful and descriptive, include the job listing and number (if there is one), and add your name.

Bcc Yourself – enter your email address on the Bcc (blind carbon copy) line so that you will receive the same email for your records and as a reminder for follow-up—the recipient won't see this in their email header.

Salutation – your greeting should address a specific person (example, Dear Mr. Mitchell)

Avoid Special Formatting – don't use bold, underlining, italics, or uncommon fonts, because they may not show up properly on the recipient's computer—keep it simple.

Body – use left justification, no centering in your email.

Find Out About Attachments – some businesses are wary of computer viruses and won't open attachments, find out if the organization wants you to attach resumes. If not, place your cover letter first and then your resume below.

Closing Line – at the end provide a closing, like "Sincerely," and below that include your typed name and contact information.

Send a Test Email – as a test, send the email to yourself first to see how it looks so that you can correct any problems before sending it to the intended recipient.

Network Contacts

Maybe your network angel can introduce you to a person they know in your field of interest. Be straightforward and ask them if they can arrange a personal introduction. If this isn't possible you can ask your network angel to send a personal note or email or to place a phone call about you to the person you want to meet. Soon after they've done this, you can call the potential employer and introduce yourself—don't wait too long or they may not remember the request.

When you call, refresh their memory about who contacted them and why. Begin by asking if it is a good time to talk (respect their time), if not ask for a better call-back time. When you do get the time to speak, explain why you're interested in their organization and what you have to offer them. If you sense that the person is really busy, keep the conversation short. But before you end the call, ask for an in-person interview.

Some people have trouble with this last bit, they don't want to impose on someone by taking up their time with an interview. Remember, "You won't get what you don't ask for."

So, go ahead, ask.

Presenting Yourself

What to Wear?

What should you wear to the interview? It depends on the job. But it is better to be overdressed than underdressed. If you're applying for a summer camp job, then nice casual would be appropriate, perhaps a nice pair of jeans or pants and a nice shirt, blouse or top. Do you have body piercings? Wear conservative studs, or leave them out altogether, and cover any large tattoos if possible.

If the position is in a conservative business environment, then for guys, a dress shirt, sports coat, tie and slacks; and for girls a conservative dress, skirt, or nice pants with a tailored blouse and jacket or sweater. The idea is for you to show them that you are professional and can fit into their environment and will dress appropriately for the job.

Speech

It's always good to know some professional terminology. If you've done your research you should be able to throw in a few job-specific vocabulary words. Every profession has its own jargon, terminology that is used in that industry to quickly get across ideas. Learn enough industry vocabulary to show that you are informed and know something about the field. (For example, if you were interested in the publishing industry the following words might come in handy: ABA—American Booksellers Association; galley—printed draft used for proofreading; deck copy—slightly smaller text under a title; backlist—older previously published books still in print; and so on.)

How you speak is very important, clear thoughtful speech is best. Don't rush your answers, questions, or comments. It's okay for there to be pauses in the conversation. And try to keep filler words to a minimum, such as "like," and avoid overly casual I'm-kicking-it-with-my-friends talk. A good rule of thumb might be that if you can't imagine it coming out of the mouth of your school principal then don't say it in an interview.

It's important to practice answering questions before going to the interview. You might enlist a friend or relative to help you practice. Have them give you a few common interviewer type questions: What special qualities can you bring to this job? What is your best strength and biggest weakness? Tell me a little about yourself. What is your passion? And so on.

After you've answered the questions, have your friend critique you. You might even make a video of yourself so that you can see how you appear to others. Body language can reveal a lot.

Do it over and over again, making improvements on your technique as you go. Keep at it until you feel reasonably comfortable and confident.

Details

Your interviewer may want to talk about practical details. Know which hours and days you are free to work (be as flexible as possible). Also, have specific questions ready that you want answered by the interviewer about the organization and the position. Your questions are also a good way of showcasing your interest and knowledge.

For example, if you were applying to work as a barista at Starbuck's, maybe you would ask about the new espresso machines they are now using and how they will improve the quality of coffee drinks, or ask about how they are incorporating more tea drinks into their menu.

Also, it's good to have a ready list of references with you. Some potential employers may want a short list of people and their contact information, maybe two or three, who know you well and can speak about your best qualities. Try not to use someone you are related to, because potential employers tend to think of them as overly biased. Past employers, teachers, counselors, ministers, scout leaders, and neighbors you've done work for would be fine. Just be sure to get their permission beforehand, update them on what you've been doing recently, and let them know someone may be calling to talk with them about you.

Tick Tock

This cannot be stressed enough: It's crucial to *be on time*! In fact, it's best to be slightly early for your meeting. This will give you a few moments to gather your thoughts and calm yourself. Know exactly where you're going before you leave home.

Making your interviewer wait for you screams disrespect and unreliability. If you can't make it to an interview on time, then what level of confidence will that person have that you will show up for work on time?

Thank You Note

After your interview be sure to send a brief thank you note to the interviewer within a day or two of your meeting. Mention the job again and that you look forward to hearing from him or her.

You can send a handwritten note or an email. Sending a thank-you shows the person that you are professional, well-mannered, and serious about the job, not to mention that it keeps your name in the forefront of the person's mind.

Another good idea is to send a note of thanks to your network angel, the person who helped you make the initial connection. People enjoy knowing the outcome of their good deeds. And you never know, you may need to ask for someone's help again someday.

You May Need a Work Permit

Once you've been offered a job, what's the next step? If you are not yet 18 and haven't graduated from high school, most states require that you have a work permit, except for volunteer or unpaid trainee positions. A work permit is a piece of paper your employer keeps on file, to show the state and school district that you have gotten the necessary legal permissions to work there.

Getting a work permit is fairly easy. You can usually go to your school administration office and request one, or sometimes the application is available online. If school is not in session, go to the office of the superintendent of schools in your city. The form will need to be completed and signed by you, your prospective employer, and your parent. Your prospective employer usually provides the following information: the job duties, maximum number of hours to be worked per day and per week, and the range of hours you will work (time of day).

Return the application to your school for their approval once you have the form completed with all the necessary signatures. Depending on the school district you live in, school officials may have specific requirements, such as a minimum grade-point average, that need to be met before they will issue a work permit. Approval of your permit is normally at your school's discretion—yet one more reason to keep those grades up. Once you've gotten the permit approved by your school, your employer is normally required to keep a copy on file.

Work Permit Exclusions

If you are self-employed, you do not need a work permit. This includes such work as babysitting, lawn mowing, or pet sitting. Being a newspaper delivery person is also usually excluded from permit requirements.

If you are an unpaid volunteer or trainee, a permit is not normally needed. However, there are certain rules that must be met for a position to qualify (find out more at *http://youthrules.dol.gov*).

Your school may be able to revoke your permit if the permit terms are violated or because of such issues as poor grades or low attendance. (In some states, your parent also has the right to cancel your permit.) Your education is a top priority. Labor laws are written in this manner to safeguard against your education suffering because of your employment situation.

Permit Expiration

In some states, work permits must be renewed every school year. Check with your school system about renewal requirements.

Work Hour Limits

Many students wonder whether there are work hour restrictions. There are federal and state limits and they vary with the student's age and whether or not the work is performed on a day when school is in session or during the summertime. On the following page, find the U.S. Department of Labor's federal restrictions on working hours for minors in non-farm employment. Note that these are federal rules and that states have their own restrictions governing youth labor hours.

State rules are typically different than federal rules. When there is a conflict between state and federal law, whichever law provides the most protection for the child will apply. To find the youth labor hour rules and permit requirements that apply to you, check online for your state's department of labor or education website.

Federal Limits by Age on Youth Working Hours in Non-Farm Employment

Age 16 to 17:

Unlimited Hours

Age 14 to 15 (School in Session):

Weekly Limit: 18 hrs per week, no working allowed during school hours

Daily Limit: 3 hrs per day on school days, including Fridays

Hours Range: 7am to 7pm Labor Day through May 31st, otherwise 7am to 9pm

Age 14 to 15 (School *not* in Session):

Weekly Limit: 40 hrs per week

Daily Limit: 8 hrs per day

Hours Range: 7am to 7pm Labor Day through May 31st, otherwise 7am to 9pm

FIGURE 2.3   The above federal restrictions are for non-agricultural employees. Internet search>> *site: dol.gov hours restrictions minors* for more details on rules. Different rules apply for state sponsored "Work Experience," "Career Exploration Program," or "Work-Study Program."

Minimum Wage

The lowest regular hourly wage allowed by law is called the minimum wage. As of January 2016, the federal minimum wage is $7.25/hr, but many states have a different minimum wage rate. The highest minimum wage applies, whether local, state or federal (in some states, some cities may have a rate even higher than the state minimum wage). For example, as of January 2016, in California the minimum wage is $10.00/hr, so the higher $10.00 rate is the law of the land in California unless local city rates are higher. To find the current minimum wage for your state you can go to the U.S. Department of Labor's website (*www.dol.gov*) and type "*state minimum wage*" in the search box.

There are some exceptions to the minimum wage law under certain programs. For example, the Youth Minimum Wage Program allows an employer to pay persons under the age of 20 a subminimum wage of $4.25/hr for a period of 90 or fewer consecutive calendar days, as long as other workers are not being displaced by the employment of the youth. After 90 days the person must be paid at least the regular minimum wage rate.

Subminimum wages are also allowed under the Full-Time Student Program (relating to students employed in retail/service stores, agriculture, or at colleges and universities) and the Student-Learner Program (relating to high school students 16 years or older enrolled in vocational education). You can do an Internet search of these terms to find the specific rules.

Recap: Getting a Job

1. Determine what you want to get from your work experience.

2. Pinpoint the field(s) in which you want to work and the types of positions you're targeting.

3. Identify and ask network angels to help you connect with someone in your area of interest.

4. Research each position, organization, and field of interest.

5. Construct a resume and cover letter for each position you're going after.

6. Make contact with your potential employer—ask for a meeting or interview.

7. Practice answering interview-type questions before an interview, use professional language.

8. Wear the appropriate clothing to the meeting or interview.

9. Be prepared for the details—references, work hours, and transportation issues.

10. Be on time for your meeting or interview.

11. Send a thank you note or email afterwards.

12. Contact your school to get a work permit, if required.

So there you have it, employment basics. Good luck!

Additional Resources

- ✓ An excellent resource about youth employment rules and regulations is *http://youthrules.dol.gov*, maintained by the Department of Labor

- ✓ To find more information on state employment laws:

  Internet search>> *site: youthrules.gov state laws*

- ✓ *www.TheBalance.com* has a lot of helpful interviewing tips—type *"youth job interview"* into the website's search box

- ✓ *Resume 101: A Student and Recent-Grad Guide to Crafting Resumes and Cover Letters That Land Jobs* by Quentin J. Schultze (Ten Speed Press, 2012) gives clear simple explanations and examples of the best ways for students to craft resumes and cover letters

- ✓ Another good book for resumes is *Best Resumes for College Students and New Grads* by Louise M. Kursmark (JIST Works, 2011)

3

Understanding Taxes and Your Paycheck

O kay, so now you have a job and you're making some money. What's next? Well, the government will be looking for its share of your earnings.

Look around you. The streets you drive on, your school, your teachers, parks you visit, patrolling police officers, and the county library you study in are all paid for with taxes.

In fact, you already pay taxes. You pay sales tax on many things that you buy (at least, in most states). The dollars you pay for food, gas, clothing, and the monthly bill for your cell phone all have taxes added on.

And now that you have earned income, the government will assume that you also owe income tax. Don't panic. The good news is that frequently teens don't make enough money in a year to owe any income tax (or the bad news, depending on how you look at it). There is a form that you can complete and submit to your employer to be used for determining how much, if any, will be deducted from your paychecks for federal income tax. It's called *Form W-4 Employee's Withholding Allowance Certificate* (W-4 for short).

Taxable and Nontaxable Income

Income is money that you receive, either earned, such as from a job, or unearned, such as from investments. This income is either taxable or nontaxable.

Taxable income includes salaries, bonuses and commissions, tips, interest income, dividend income, realized capital gains (increases in value of stocks or bonds when sold), and unemployment compensation.

Nontaxable income includes things like cash rebates, worker's compensation benefits, welfare, gifts, and most life insurance proceeds.

Income Tax Withholding and Your Wages

When an employer holds back a portion of an employee's wages for taxes, it is called *withholding*. The government requires employers to withhold part of the earnings of most employees and to transmit the withheld amount to the *Internal Revenue Service* (IRS) and the state's taxing authority for states that collect income tax. These withholdings are counted towards paying for the employee's expected income taxes owed for that year.

The IRS, which is the federal agency responsible for administering America's federal income tax system, has created Form W-4 to assist employers and employees in determining the proper withholding amount. When you complete a W-4 and submit it to your employer you are giving your employer the information needed to calculate how much money to withhold for taxes from your earnings each pay period, money which they will then send to the government.

There is a similar form for determining withholding of state income taxes. (In California it's called Form DE 4—each state has its own version.) Usually, if you complete a W-4 the same withholding information is used for calculating state income tax withholding. You can check online to find the rules for your state taxing authority (note: a few states don't collect state income tax).

Why Withholdings Are Important

You want the amount withheld from your earnings to be as close as possible to your income tax obligation for that year—not too little and not too much (kind of like Goldilocks searching for the right size chair). If too much has been withheld, you will need to file an income tax return to get a *refund* for that year. And if too little has been withheld (meaning, you've under withheld), then you will need to pay more money to the government when you file your income tax return.

If income taxes have been greatly under withheld from your earnings you may have to pay a penalty fee to the IRS (see *www.irs.gov/taxtopics/tc306.html* for the details). Generally speaking, you fall into the penalty range if your income taxes are under withheld by $1,000 or more, *and* your withholdings covered less than 90% of your income tax obligation for that year, *and* your total withholdings for the year are less than 100% of your prior year's income tax obligation.

The under-withholding penalty must be paid in addition to the taxes you owe the IRS when filing your return (Form 2210 is used to calculate the penalty amount). It's best to fill out and submit a W-4 as accurately as possible to ensure that your employer withholds the proper amount for income tax from your regular earnings.

The Self-Employed and Estimated Taxes

Self-employed individuals who expect to owe $1,000 or more in taxes for a given year usually need to file *estimated taxes* (see *IRS Publication 505*), as a substitute for employer withholding, on their self-employment income. Estimated taxes are payments made directly to the IRS, instead of through an employer, and are usually made in four installments throughout the year—typically paid by the 15th of April, June, September, and January. (*Form 1040-ES, Estimated Tax for Individuals,* is used to calculate payments.)

Just like with employee withholdings, if insufficient estimated tax payments are made, the taxpayer may be required to pay a penalty.

Determining Withholdings

When you start a paying job you will have the opportunity to fill out a W-4, which your employer will use to determine how much to hold back from your wages for the payment of income taxes. The form can be obtained from your employer or you can print one directly from the IRS's website at *www.irs.gov*.

It's possible you may not need to pay any income taxes at all (this is called being *exempt* from withholdings). There are specific requirements that need to be met in order to qualify for this status. The limits and rules are subject to change yearly. (You can see IRS Publication 505 online to determine if you qualify.)

As an example, in 2015 you would probably have qualified as exempt from withholdings if all of the following had been true: 1) you could have been claimed as a dependent on an adult's tax return; 2) you had $6,300 or less in earned income; 3) you had $350 or less in unearned income (such as interest income or capital gains); and 4) you didn't have to pay income tax in the prior year. The IRS website gives a complete list of the current requirements.

If you qualify for exempt status, there is a line on the W-4 form where you can write the word "Exempt." Completing the rest of the form is simple. You will supply your name, marital status, social security number, address, and sign the document. The completed form is submitted to your employer. If you properly file as exempt, there should be no withholdings for federal income tax.

The exempt status expires every year in mid-February. If you were eligible for exemption and then were still eligible the following year, you would need to file a new W-4 with your employer by February 15th to ensure that they would continue to not withhold federal income taxes from your paycheck.

If you don't qualify as exempt, you can use the Personal Allowance Worksheet at the top of Form W-4 to help you figure your *withholding allowances*.

Withholding Allowances *

Think of withholding allowances as the government's way of "allowing" you to reduce the amount of money to be withheld from your wages because of personal circumstances that are expected to reduce your tax bill, such as being the primary financial support for others or having a lot of *tax deductions*.

Tax Deductions

Our tax laws permit some types of taxpayer expenses in certain situations to be subtracted from a taxpayer's taxable income. These reductions are called tax deductions.

Such expenses as charitable donations, home mortgage interest payments, and property taxes paid, can typically be used, all or in part, as tax deductions.

By decreasing taxable income a taxpayer lowers the amount of income tax she owes.

For example, a single parent supporting a child should have more allowances than a person who is single with no children all other things being equal. Under current tax law, the single parent is permitted more of a tax break given the added expense of supporting a child. The individual would most likely use the *filing status* of "Head of Household."

Filing Status

A taxpayer's filing status is a designation used to categorize income tax filers. The filing status impacts how much tax the filer has to pay—it affects the filer's allowable credits and deductions. The four most common filing statuses are 1) Single, 2) Married Filing Jointly, 3) Married Filing Separately, and 4) Head of Household.

Most unmarried students would file as "Single" (to determine your filing status, Internet search>> *site: irs.gov filing status*).

Claiming allowances on your W-4 decreases the amount of money withheld from your paycheck by your employer. The IRS provides an online calculator to help taxpayers determine their correct withholding allowances (Internet search>> *site: irs.gov withholding calculator*).

An employer who doesn't receive a W-4 from their employee must withhold income tax as if the employee had filed a W-4 with zero allowances and with the filing status of "Single." This requires that the maximum withholding rate be applied. The employee can later file a tax return and get a refund if too much has been withheld.

If You Have Multiple Jobs

When you have more than one employer, a W-4 form needs to be completed for each. To help earners with two or more jobs to have the right amount withheld, there is a worksheet on the back of each W-4 form. In addition to this Two-Earners/Multiple Jobs Worksheet, taxpayers can also use the IRS withholding calculator mentioned earlier.

Where to See Your Withholdings

The Department of Labor requires employers to keep accurate payroll records for each employee. The records include the employee name, social security number, dates covered by each pay period, total hours worked, number of overtime hours, earnings, and deductions from earnings for tax withholdings and other items like health insurance and retirement plan contributions.

Employers must provide their employees with access to these pay statements either as printed documents or by online means. In addition, after the close of the year employees should receive a W-2 *Wage and Tax Statement* from their employers.

Social Security and Medicare Taxes

Social Security and Medicare are funded by taxes. Social Security is a federal pension program and Medicare provides medical insurance for older individuals. They both fall under the Federal Insurance Contribution Act (FICA).

Most workers are required to pay Social Security and Medicare taxes, and their employers must withhold money accordingly, just like for income taxes. However, students working for their college or university while attending school might be exempt from having to pay these FICA taxes (check with the school student employment office).

What a W-2 Statement Shows

The W-2 statement is a yearend federal tax document that states the total amount of money an employee has earned for a given year at a given job, and also what was subtracted from the individual's earnings. Think of it as a summation of the employee's periodic pay statements for that year.

Employers must provide virtually every paid employee with a W-2, even if the employee has claimed exemption from withholding on their W-4 form. You should receive your W-2 each year by January 31st for your prior year's earnings. If you haven't received one by then, contact your employer.

There are a series of boxes on the W-2 statement numbered "1" through "20" and another set of boxes labeled "a" through "f." The lettered boxes mostly supply basic information about you and your job—for example, your name, social security number, and place of employment. Information related to your earnings, withholding, and employment status can be found in the numbered boxes. Most of the figures in the boxes correspond to dollar amounts, some boxes may be empty. The numbered boxes are where you look to see your total compensation, federal and state income tax withheld, and Social Security tax and Medicare tax withheld for the year. (Visit *www.irs.gov* to see what an actual W-2 form looks like.)

Getting a Tax Refund

If money is being withheld from your earnings for income taxes and you think too much has been withheld for the year, you may be eligible for a tax refund. To determine if you are owed money and how much, you will need to complete a tax return for that year.

The majority of U.S. taxpayers now file electronically. And for 2015 if you had *adjusted gross income* (AGI) of $62,000 or less, you can use brand-name commercial tax software for free to help you file your 2015 taxes. This program, which began in 2003, is called *Free File*. It is an arrangement that the federal government has with an alliance of software companies to assist income tax filers who have AGI below a given level (the income limit changes each year). To get started, go to the IRS website (*www.irs.gov/freefile*).

Once you start the Free File process at the website, you will be given a list of several tax software companies to choose from. When you select one you can click on their link to be taken to the company website and then walked through the filing process. Some software companies will also compute your state income tax for free or for a fee.

Even if you make more than the low-income limit, you can still file IRS forms electronically using their *Free File Fillable Forms* online, but you won't have access to the free commercial software to help you through the filing process. Also, the forms cannot be used for state income tax preparation.

Income Tax Returns

Income tax returns are the forms taxpayers complete once a year and file with federal and state taxing authorities. These forms require information about taxpayer income, tax deductions, filing status, and other information used to compute income tax.

For federal returns taxpayers file either IRS Form 1040, 1040A, or 1040EZ. Which form is used is determined by how much money a taxpayer earned, the source of that income, and other considerations. Form 1040 is the most complicated and Form 1040EZ is the simplest. (See *IRS Publication 17: Tax Guide for Individuals* about requirements for using the various IRS returns.)

State tax returns vary. (A few states don't even require state income tax.) Check online to find the filing requirements for your state.

Adjusted Gross Income

A lower adjusted gross income (AGI) can reduce the amount of income tax you owe. AGI is a line item on your income tax return that is calculated as gross income minus adjustments to gross income. Deductions from gross income are for specific expenses, such as student loan interest payments or certain retirement account contributions. IRS rules limit under what circumstances these adjustments can be made and the amounts allowed.

Income Tax Filing Deadline

Tax returns are due April 15th of the year following when the income was earned. If April 15th falls on a weekend then the due date shifts to the following Monday. For example, if you are filing a tax return for the year 2015 then you need to have your tax return in the mail and postmarked by April 15th of 2016, or transmitted by midnight of April 15th for e-filed returns.

If for some reason you can't make the filing deadline, you can apply for an automatic six-month extension using IRS *Form 4868*. However, you should still pay by April 15th what you think you owe in taxes, because the IRS can charge you interest for any taxes unpaid after the April 15th deadline has passed.

Unfortunately, interest doesn't work in reverse—if the IRS owes you a refund they won't pay you interest on the refunded amount.

Recap: Taxes and Your Paycheck

1. When you start a paying job, get Form W-4 from your employer or online at *www.irs.gov*.

2. See if you qualify for exemption from withholding by visiting *www.irs.gov* for *Publication 505: Tax Withholding*.

3. If you don't qualify for exemption, use the worksheets on Form W-4 to calculate withholdings or use the IRS calculator.

4. Return a completed W-4 to your employer, regardless of whether or not you are exempt from withholdings. Complete one for each job.

5. Review your tax situation at the beginning of every year and submit a new W-4 if you need to adjust your withholding allowances.

6. If you qualify as exempt from withholding this year and continue to qualify the next year, then you need to submit a new W-4 by February 15th of the next year to maintain your exempt status.

7. At the beginning of every year look for your Form W-2. Contact your employer in early February if you don't receive a W-2 by January 31st.

8. Tax returns are due April 15th. (Even if you don't owe any tax, you may be due a refund.)

9. Keep copies of your W-2(s) and tax return(s) each year for your records.

Additional Resources

- ✓ IRS Publication 505 explains withholding rules and estimated tax payments. Go to *www.irs.gov/publications*

- ✓ For help with figuring correct W-4 withholdings try:

  Internet search>> *site: irs.gov withholding calculator*

  Internet search>> *site: paycheckcity.com W-4 calculator*

- ✓ For information on e-filing:

  Internet search>> *site: irs.gov Free File*

- ✓ To download a copy of Form W-4 withholding certificate:

  Internet search>> *site: irs.gov form w-4 pdf*

- ✓ For information on filing status:

  Internet search>> *site: irs.gov filing status*

- ✓ *Taxes Made Simple: Income Taxes Explained in 100 Pages or Less* by Mike Piper (Simple Subjects, 2014) provides a good uncomplicated overview of federal income taxes

4

Creating a Spending Plan

Have you ever drawn up an elaborate exercise and diet plan as a New Year's resolution? You spell out what exercises you will do every day and for how many minutes, the foods you will eat, the rewards you will give yourself, and on and on. It's very difficult to keep up such a tight schedule. Messing up just one day can throw your whole schedule off track. And after a few screw-ups you might throw in the towel and say forget it.

People naturally resist strict controls on their behavior, especially when it comes to something as much fun as spending money—it's so much more thrilling to spend it than to keep track of it! Unfortunately, constantly spending on a whim can keep you from achieving your financial goals, and can leave you tied up with lots of debt.

The spending plan outlined in the rest of this chapter is relatively simple. With this plan you first decide how much of your monthly income you want to allocate to the areas most important to you, put that money aside into different buckets, and then use the remainder as your discretionary spending to do with as you like. And it doesn't require much math, just the basics—a little addition, subtraction, and division.

Starting with an uncomplicated strategy will greatly improve your chance of success in maintaining your plan. Learning to manage the flow of your money, the controlled making and spending of it, is one of the most important financial management skills you can learn.

Benefits of a Spending Plan

Why bother with a spending plan? What will it get you?

First of all, it allows you to control your spending instead of your spending controlling you. When your spending is out of whack you can find yourself teetering on the edge of going broke, waiting for your next paycheck to pay off last month's bills, sweating every decision that requires money because you don't know if the funds will be there when you need them. That's no way to live.

Second, if you want to save for something expensive, like a car, a spending plan will get you there much faster than haphazard saving.

Third, if you have a credit card, being able to control your spending will help keep you off the nerve-racking *debt* merry-go-round, which many adults find themselves on, facing growing credit card balances that take years to pay off.

And last, it encourages you to periodically consider what you want to be doing with your life in the near future and the long-term—to do some life planning.

Debt

Financial debt is an obligation, taken on by a person or an organization, to repay money that has been borrowed. This debt normally includes interest charges and fees related to the debt.

Common types of debt that an individual might have are a mortgage (money borrowed to buy a house, or other real estate), an auto loan (money borrowed to purchase a car), or credit card debt (money borrowed by making purchases with a credit card).

Building a Spending Plan

What follows is an eight-step process for creating and maintaining a spending plan:

1. Determine your monthly income (after taxes and other payroll deductions, if any).

2. Decide on how much money you want to have available for important unexpected opportunities, emergencies, and your long-term future and then the portion of your monthly income you are willing to save towards these.

3. Decide on specific short-term and mid-term goals you want to achieve and their cost and the amount that you want to set aside for them every month.

4. Determine how much of your monthly income is needed for ongoing commitments, like a cell phone bill or gasoline expense.

5. Consider what is left as the discretionary spending portion of your income.

6. Segregate your money into different saving buckets according to these spending requirements and see if you can follow your plan every month.

7. Make adjustments if you find you can't maintain your monthly estimated spending streams — revise your goals, and/or scale back your commitments, and/or cut your discretionary spending, and/or earn more income.

8. Revisit your spending plan every six months, or when there are major changes in your life, and update your goals and commitments.

That's it.

Next, let's discuss the mechanics of these steps using some hypothetical numbers.

Income

Your income is all the money that you earn or receive every month. For the purpose of creating a spending plan, assume that income means money earned after any taxes withheld or other payroll deductions have been applied. Sources could be from a regular job, odd jobs, allowances, gifts, or whatever. In this hypothetical situation, let's say that you mow lawns on weekends, which provides you with $200 a month. You also get $40 a month for doing chores around the house and make $60 a month babysitting. Total that and you have $300 worth of income every month.

Next, let's look at what you plan to save.

Putting Yourself First – Self-Investment Savings

Okay, what's the single most important monetary commitment you have? Yourself, a financial commitment to yourself. This is the notion behind *pay yourself first*. You should first set aside some of your income for your future. This is so important that it has a special name in this book: *My Self-Investment* (MSI) savings.

What will you use these MSI savings for? Perhaps there is a life-changing event on your horizon somewhere, but you just don't know what it is yet. And it may require money. Maybe you'll have the opportunity to study abroad someday, and you'll need $1,500 immediately, or maybe you'll have the chance to do a summer research job important to your college major, but the job doesn't pay anything, so you'll need $1,200 for living expenses. Who knows what may come up? The point is that there may be key opportunities that you don't want to miss. Having money set aside may allow you to take advantage of these once-in-a-lifetime events.

Another use for MSI savings is preparing for your retirement. Yes, it's a long way off, but opening a retirement account early and making regular contributions to it makes building a large retirement savings reserve infinitely easier. (We'll talk more about retirement accounts in a later chapter.)

There is also occasionally the unexpected mishap. What if you drop your smartphone, break the glass, and it needs to be replaced? Your MSI savings can help cover things like this also.

Start by putting aside at least 10% to 20% of your income to build your MSI savings. In this example, $30 a month (10% of $300) goes towards your MSI savings.

Goals Savings

Dream a little. What do you want that you can't afford right now? Perhaps concert tickets, a new computer, or maybe you want a car. These are things that you can't pay for right now but could save enough money for in one to three years to purchase them. We'll call these your *goals savings*.

In this example, let's say you want a new tablet computer that costs $420. You also want to have $1,200 in your bank account when you go off to college.

It will be 30 months before you start college. Take $1,200 divided over 30 months to figure the set-aside amount of $40 per month. You've also decided to wait 12 months to purchase the tablet, so that's $35 a month to be saved ($420 divided by 12 months). Altogether, you need to save $75 a month for these goals ($40 for college and $35 for the computer).

Commitments – Regular Spending

Now, consider what important expenses you regularly pay for every month. Think of things that would make life difficult if you had to do without them, things you need. These are your regular *commitments*.

For this example, we'll say that you pay $50 a month for your portion of the family cell phone contract, $60 a month to refill the family car with gas, and $10 a month in maintenance and gas expense for the mower. That's $120 a month in total commitments.

Next, consider periodic expenses, such as an annual or quarterly bill. These expenditures might include things like membership dues, annual subscription fees, or semi-annual insurance payments. Think back over the past year or go through your bank account activity for the last 12 months to pinpoint these kind of expenditures.

These can be factored into your plan by estimating periodic costs for the entire year and then dividing the total by 12 to get a monthly expenditure number. Some months you may have surplus savings if you haven't actually paid for the periodic expense yet. And that's okay because you will keep the money in your account and let it build up until it is time to pay that bill.

Periodic Expenses

Periodic expenditures are paid quarterly, semi-annually, annually, or some other infrequent recurring period. These may be things like an annual car registration fee or annual membership dues, expenses which are easy to overlook when putting together a spending plan.

Discretionary Spending

Whatever remains, after you have figured your MSI savings, goals savings, and commitments, is discretionary money. This is money you can choose to spend however you like. It is not set aside for any specific purpose. In this example the remainder is $75 a month out of the $300 of income.

Putting Together Your Spending Plan

Organize your numbers in a table, like the one in Figure 4.1, and calculate what percentage of income you would allocate to each spending area. Each category's percentage of total income is determined by dividing your planned category spending by your estimated total monthly income (see column four in Figure 4.1).

In this example, your income is $300 a month and you put $30 away for MSI savings (10%), $75 for goals savings (25%), $120 for commitments (40%), and $75 is left over for discretionary spending (25%).

Once you have the percentages you can apply them to any income dollar amount and calculate the planned spending amount for a given category. For example, if your income turns out to be $360, $60 more than projected, you can still use the same percentages to allocate your money by category: $36 for MSI savings (10%), $90 for goal savings (25%), $144 for commitments (40%), and $90, the remainder, for discretionary spending (25%). You'll put away more money than expected, but that's okay because next month's income may be lower than expected. If your estimates were fairly accurate, it should all even out after a while.

If you are chronically short of discretionary funds every month, you may want to take another look at your plan. Perhaps you need to reassess your savings. For instance, in our hypothetical example maybe the goal of $35 for a computer is too high a number. You could revise it to $25 a month and free up $10 for something else. Of course, this means it will take almost five months longer to purchase the computer. It's a tradeoff.

Or perhaps, you've overestimated your income or maybe underestimated your regular commitments. Your spending may not work out perfectly as planned at first.

Whatever the reason, try tweaking your plan a bit here and there until you have something you can live with. It is a back and forth process and may take a bit of time before you to come up with workable numbers.

Any plan, even if not perfect, is better than no plan at all. The act of planning itself is the first step in getting control of your spending. And once you have control you can consciously direct where you want your money to go.

It's best to divide your category money into separate accounts or in some other way so that you know how much money is allocated to what. One method would be to keep the commitments money in a checking account, where you could easily access money as needed to pay these expenses; the MSI savings and goals savings money could be kept in a savings account, and you could keep a written record of how much belongs to each; and the discretionary spending could be kept as cash at home somewhere safe. The important thing is to create a system of buckets for segregating your money.

Spending Plan

Category	Monthly Income or (Expense)	Percent of Income	Formula
Income	$300	100%	
MSI Savings	($30)	10%	(10% = $30/$300)
Goals Savings	($75)	25%	(25% = $75/$300)
Commitments	($120)	40%	(40% = $120/$300)
Discretionary Spending	($75)	25%	(25% = $75/$300)
Total	($300)	100%	

FIGURE 4.1

Stretching Your Dollars

Sometimes just spending more consciously will solve a cash flow problem. Here are some dollar-stretching ideas:

- Before going shopping make up a shopping list with estimated dollar amounts you're going to spend and then stick to it. Only bring enough money to buy what you've planned for (including sales tax).

- Don't buy something just because it's "on sale" or is a "good deal"—the price isn't really cheap if you don't need it and can't afford it.

- Choose a lower-price cell phone plan. (Can you use a cheaper data plan?) If your parents pay the cell phone bill and you can live with a less expensive plan, maybe they would be willing to add some of the savings to your allowance.

- Brownbag lunch more often. Ask your parents to grocery shop for specific foods for making lunches.

- Cut back on expensive specialty food items, like coffee drinks and smoothies—try getting up five minutes earlier and make yourself a cup of tea or coffee at home.

- Shop at thrift stores sometimes, garage sales, or on eBay.

- Don't carry a lot of extra money around, just what you need for that day—spare money tends to burn a hole in a pocket.

Other people can also be very helpful in creating income opportunities or assist in economizing on your spending. For example, if you're saving for something specific explain your plan to your parents; maybe they will have some extra work around the house they'd be happy to turn over to you in exchange for giving you extra funds. Likewise, if you let it be known that you're saving for something, neighbors may have odd yard jobs, pet-sitting, or babysitting jobs for you.

Your friends might even be willing to help by eating lunch more often on campus with you or being understanding about choosing less expensive entertainment activities if you tell them what you're saving for. Who knows, once they see your success, they might even be inspired to create their own spending plans.

Future Adjustments

Your spending plan is not fixed—it shouldn't weigh you down like cement shoes. As you age, your needs will change and they'll get more complicated. You'll drop goals and add new ones, you'll graduate, probably go to college, get a permanent job, and perhaps buy a car. Who knows? Each of these shifts in your life can mean significant changes in your financial situation.

Your concerns in high school may be very different from those you'll have in college. Likewise, when you're working fulltime you'll probably have different goals than as a college student. Your priorities will reorder: new smartphone versus apartment deposit, trip to the beach versus a semester studying abroad, new video games versus a bedspread and sheets.

Once you've created a plan, you'll want to revisit it from time to time. Look at it every six months or so to see if it still makes sense for you. As you get older and take on more responsibility, your income will likely increase, as will your commitment spending and the scope of your goals. You'll probably want different and more detailed categories and to set up other financial accounts. But the basic concept for creating a spending plan is still the same.

You can make your spending plan as simple or as intricate as you like. The plan presented here is just one way of creating one—there are lots of other methods. No matter what system you choose, the idea is still the same—you *first* put away money for future savings, goals, and commitments, and then fund your discretionary spending.

The point is to have some kind of a plan to follow, no matter how simple or complicated. It's important to have a roadmap for your finances and to use it. Now is a great time to get in the habit of directing the flow of your money.

Recap: Creating a Spending Plan

1. Determine your average monthly income—include money from jobs, allowances, and self-employment ventures.

2. Figure out how much to put aside for My Self-Investment (MSI) savings each month—always have money earmarked for your future and emergencies. Start by saving at least 10% to 20% of your income.

3. Decide what specific goals you want to achieve and when, then calculate how much you want to save for them each month.

4. Determine what your monthly spending commitments are—important regular expenses. (Turn infrequent commitments into regular monthly expenses by saving for them over 12 months.)

5. Put it all together in a written plan showing what your allocation percentages are for each spending category.

6. Use these allocation percentages every week or month to divide up your income according to your plan. Set up separate accounts and/or keep detailed records.

7. Revisit your plan periodically to make adjustments to it as your life situation changes.

Additional Resources

✓ These sites have good budgeting worksheets:

Internet search>> *site: kiplinger.com household budget worksheet*

Internet search>> *site: financialliteracymonth.com expense worksheet*

Internet search>> *site: moneyandstuff.info budget worksheets*

✓ For a discussion of useful budgeting apps for young adults:

Internet search>> *site: nerdwallet.com budgeting apps for new-grad*

✓ A good online free resource for setting up and automating a spending plan and tracking transactions can be found at www.*mint.com*

5

Understanding How Credit Scores Work

C redit (debt) seems to be the media's favorite villain these days. Headlines in news stories repeatedly remind us of how consumers are drowning in credit card debt, college students and parents are suffocating under the weight of student loans, and homeowners are over extended on their mortgages.

While all of this is true, credit can also be useful when handled wisely. Like money, credit is not fundamentally good or bad, it's how people use it that matters.

The majority of people, at some point will choose to borrow money to purchase something expensive that they otherwise would not have been able to afford right away, such as a house. When you use credit, you are agreeing to pay for something over a period of time rather than all at once. You are borrowing money from an institution or individual and paying it back with interest. Interest being the expense you pay for borrowing the money.

Banks and other financial institutions consider several key elements when deciding how much interest to charge on a loan. Details like how much money is being borrowed, how long it is being borrowed for, and what is being purchased with the money are all part of the equation. One other important factor a lender weighs is the borrower's past credit behavior, good or bad.

Your Credit Report and Score

If you have participated in certain types of financial transactions, like using a credit card or making payments on a loan in your name, then you likely have a credit history. This credit history is comprised of your credit-related actions over time and is summarized in a document called a *credit report*.

You probably don't have credit cards or loans in your name yet, so you aren't likely to have a credit report. Nevertheless, this chapter provides important material that may help you in the not too distant future.

Businesses such as banks and other finance companies report consumer credit balances and activity to *credit* bureaus. The bureaus maintain this data, along with the related individual's name and social security number. Data collected includes such information as on-time and late account payments, account balances, account closings, credit limits, new credit cards applied for, and loan activity. Credit reports are issued by the bureaus.

This credit data is the basis for a person's *credit score*, the score being a numerical representation of the credit report. The more responsibly an individual handles his or her credit— making loan payments on time and not over borrowing, and so on—then the higher the credit score and the lower the interest rate on loans that lenders are likely to offer that person.

A favorable credit score can save an individual thousands of dollars in interest payments over the life of a large loan. No small consideration when you're looking to purchase something expensive like a home.

Credit Bureaus

Credit bureaus are companies that maintain databases on people's credit related activities. There are three major credit bureaus, TransUnion, Equifax, and Experian. They collect data about the credit activity of individuals by name and social security number. Finance companies and other businesses regularly report information to these bureaus about credit card accounts and loans that they administer. Loan information tracked includes student, auto, and home loans. All of this information becomes part of an individual's credit history.

A good credit score is like a helpful letter of introduction to the world; it can open doors for you. However, a poor credit score can be like an unfavorable reference you have to overcome to get where you want to go. When it comes to buying a car, leasing an apartment, buying a house, applying for a job, getting insurance, getting a cell phone contract, and in many other situations, having a good credit history can smooth your way.

People with high credit scores are the ones that snag those zero-percent financing deals that car companies love to dangle in front of consumers. Your credit score is a gauge, a way for businesses to quickly assess whether or not you can handle your financial obligations responsibly. It's nothing personal, just business.

Credit Score

A person's credit score is derived from the individual's credit report. It is a calculated number based on a series of formulas. The most common credit score is called the FICO score and ranges from 300 to 850. It is maintained by the Fair Isaac Corporation.

The higher the score the better. Businesses review a person's credit score when deciding on such things as whether to offer a person a credit card or a loan, and on what terms.

There are a series of mathematical calculations (more on this later) that are performed on the data in your credit report to determine your credit score. You actually have several credit scores, some are tailored to specific industries like mortgage lending and auto financing. And not every credit bureau collects the same information on you. They each have a slightly different set of data.

The FICO scoring system is the most widely used. FICO is an acronym for the Fair Isaac Corporation, the company that created and maintains the scoring system and scores. The standard FICO score ranges from 300 to 850. The higher your score the better; it means you look more appealing to lenders. And lenders offer the lowest interest rates on loans to their most favored customers. In addition, a higher credit score may help ease the way when it comes to applying for an apartment lease, dealing with insurance companies, and sometimes even when applying for jobs.

Now, let's move on to how credit scores are calculated.

How to Maintain and Build a Favorable Score

A FICO score of 850 is sterling and only a small segment of the population achieves it. Most people never attain a perfect score, but there are things that you can do to improve your score and keep it up.

There are five main factors used in determining a credit score, the breakdown is as follows:

FICO Scoring Factors	Percentage Weighting
Payment History	35%
Length of History	15%
Amount Owed	30%
New Credit Inquiries	10%
Type of Credit Held	10%
Total	100%

FIGURE 5.1 The higher the percentage weighting, the more significance it has in calculating the FICO score.

Following is an explanation of each of the scoring factors shown in Figure 5.1:

Payment History – 35%

With a weighting of 35%, this is the single most important factor in determining your credit score. You'll want to pay extra attention to this area. Payment History concerns such things as how often you've made credit card and loan payments on time, as well as the amounts, and how many, if any, of your payments were late and the number of days they were late and the amounts involved.

Having delinquent debt (late payments) on your record can damage your score. It's important to make payments on time, and if you miss the due date, to pay as soon as you can. (If you're payment is less than 30 days late, lenders typically do not report it to credit bureaus.)

Length of History – 15%

This refers to how long your various accounts have been open and the time since your last account activity. This factor has a 15% weighting. This is why some credit experts say that consumers should think twice before closing a long-standing credit card account. (Although, closing an account may become a priority for those who are constantly tempted to overspend.) Also, occasionally using credit card accounts keeps them active and discourages credit card companies from closing them because of inactivity.

Amount Owed – 30%

Here is another critical factor. It is weighted 30% and concerns how many accounts you have with balances, how much you owe in total on all of your accounts, and the amount of credit that is available to you. What is being examined is the *debt utilization ratio*, the amount of credit available to you that you are using. For example, if you have a $1,000 credit limit on a credit card and you currently owe $200 on that card, then the utilization ratio on that account is 20% ($200 divided by $1,000).

Keeping utilization ratios low will help your credit score, as will not having an excessive number of credit accounts in your name. Potential lenders get nervous when a consumer has a lot of credit accounts at his or her disposal, accounts where large debt balances could quickly materialize.

New Credit Inquiries – 10%

This factor is less critical but still affects your score. A rapid series of credit account openings is considered a negative, as well as frequently having lenders review your *credit report* (called a credit inquiry), such as if you are shopping around for a loan.

If you are looking for a car at various dealerships, or for another expensive item, and you want to see if you qualify for a loan and on what terms, try to complete your comparison shopping within a 45-day window. Why? Because credit inquiries made within this timeframe are usually counted as only one inquiry, instead of several. (Companies often want to review a consumer's credit report before giving estimates for loan rates and payment schedules.)

Type of Credit Held – 10%

This one is relatively straight forward—variety adds spice to your credit score. Having different types of accounts (such as credit card, auto loan, and home loan) in good standing is usually seen as a positive. However, it is only weighted 10%, so don't worry too much about this one. It's better to not overdo it—only open accounts you actually need.

Review Your Credit Report for Errors

The last step in maintaining a healthy credit report is to review it for mistakes every year and, if any are found, to get them corrected. Mistakes happen more frequently than most people realize. Once a year you can get a free copy of your credit report from each of the three major credit bureaus by going to *www.annualcreditreport.com*.

Your credit report does not show your credit score (you can pay a credit bureau to get your score). What the report details is information such as financial account names and numbers, type of accounts, longevity of accounts, payment histories, balances, limits, addresses, and so on. You can go through the report to check for errors. If you find any, you can write the credit bureau to get it corrected. Sometimes you may need to follow up with additional correspondences to see that corrections are made properly.

If you stagger your requests by asking for one free report from a different bureau every four months, then in a year's time you will have received a good overview of your entire credit history. You can repeat this process every year. Doing this will allow you to catch errors that may pop up in your reports and to keep an eye out for fraud.

Recap: Credit Scores

1. A higher credit score can help you obtain lower interest rates on loans, which can save you thousands of dollars over your lifetime.

2. Landlords, cell phone companies, insurance companies, and even potential employers (with your permission) will sometimes use your credit score to help evaluate you.

3. Your credit score is based on your credit history, it reflects your debt management skills—things like whether or not you can make on-time payments and how much of your available credit you use.

4. If you have credit accounts, you can review your credit history every year by getting a free copy of your credit report.

5. Look for errors on the credit report and get them corrected, and also watch for signs of identity theft, which need to be reported.

Additional Resources

✓ For more information on credit reports and credit scores, visit these websites:

Internet search>> *site: fdic.gov credit report basics*

Internet search>> *site: consumer.ftc.gov topics credit and loans*

✓ Get a free copy of your credit report from each of the three major credit bureaus once a year at *www.annualcreditreport.com*

6

Using Credit Cards Intelligently

O n college campuses across America in the early 80s, getting a credit card as a student was unbelievably easy. Kiosks on campuses peppered the main quad and other student gathering areas, looking like concession stands at a state fair. Each booth offered a different enticement—a free T-shirt, stuffed animals, a keychain or some other prize—for a student to come and complete a credit card application.

Unfortunately, as time passed, many college students fell deep into credit card debt. A 2009 study of "How Undergraduates Use Credit Cards" conducted by Sallie Mae found that of the students they surveyed the average credit card debt was over $3,000.

Fortunately, this trend has started to reverse itself in recent years, no doubt in part because of the passage of the *Credit Card Act of 2009*. This act was written partly to address this growing problem among students. The act created new rules about how and when college students could be marketed to by credit card companies. Now, marketing done by credit card companies is limited in proximity to college campus borders, and there are rules concerning young people under the age of 21 opening credit card accounts.

Still, far too many people treat credit cards as an extra source of income. Consumers too often ignore the fact that credit card debt is basically a loan that has to be repaid at some point and that until it is interest is charged on the *outstanding balance* (money owed to the credit card company).

Credit Card Interest

When you use a credit card to pay for goods or services, the finance company pays the merchants for you and then sends you a bill every month for all of the purchases you made. If you don't pay the full amount of the bill, the finance company will apply interest to any unpaid money and add it to your account balance for the next month.

Interest charges are recalculated every month on any unpaid balance until everything is paid off. For example, if a $300 balance remains after you make your payment on a credit card bill and the interest rate is 2% per month, then interest of $6 will be added to the $300 balance. This creates a new higher outstanding balance of $306 for the following month. And if you continue to make purchases with the card, then those will also be added in to create an even higher balance.

(Note: this example is an oversimplification because finance companies often charge interest on a *daily* basis, which makes the credit card balance grow even faster.)

Having credit cards can be a negative or a positive experience. It's all about how you handle them. Misuse of credit cards can leave you deeply in debt. Credit cards can be used to reinforce expensive impulse buying habits, and reckless usage can seriously damage your credit score.

On the other hand, if you learn to use credit cards wisely they can help you build a good credit history, be a great source of emergency funds, and be convenient when cash isn't an option. Having a good credit history and score can mean that businesses will offer you credit and on better terms. Before using credit cards it's important to understand how they work and how best to use and not abuse them.

How Credit Cards Work

When you open a credit card account you are given a card with your name and a unique multi-digit number, which you can use to make purchases. In essence, you are provided the freedom to borrow money, up to a predetermined maximum amount, from the finance company at a given rate of interest. Everything is great as far as the finance company is concerned as long as you continue to make the minimum required monthly payments on the account balance and you don't exceed the card's *credit limit* (the contractual debt limit of the credit card account).

Credit card accounts are known as *revolving debt* because you can borrow money indefinitely, month after month, as long as you make the minimum monthly payments and don't exceed your credit limit. (Think of a person going in and out of a revolving door, over and over again.) The details of the card are spelled out in the *credit card agreement*. It should be reviewed carefully.

Credit Card Agreement

It is a document specifying the contractual terms and conditions for using the credit card. Spelled out in the agreement is important information about such things as payment due dates, grace periods, and penalty policies. A copy of the agreement is typically mailed along with your initial credit card, in addition finance companies normally have agreements posted on their websites.

Below are some important features to understand before signing up for a credit card:

Interest Rate

When you borrow money from an organization you are normally charged interest. Interest is typically calculated as a percentage of the money borrowed. Interest is the periodic cost of borrowing money until the lender has been repaid. Some credit cards have a fixed rate of interest and other cards a variable rate of interest (commonly tied to some widely published fluctuating interest rate). Whatever means are used, the lower the rate the better for the consumer.

The interest rate on the card is applied to the outstanding balance, money you owe the credit card company. If you don't pay off your balance in full every month, the balance becomes like a continuous loan on which interest is being charged until you get the balance back to zero.

Rates on credit cards can be quite high (rates of 17% interest on up are not uncommon), so it's best not to carry a balance. And if your payment is late or you exceed your borrowing limit on the card, the finance company may increase your interest rate in the future.

If you pay off your card balance faithfully every month by the due date, with most credit cards you won't be charged any interest. It is like getting a free short-term loan.

Minimum Payment

If, for some reason, one month you don't pay off your full balance, you must pay at least a minimum required amount or a penalty fee will be added to your account balance. The required minimum is typically either a percentage of the outstanding balance, such as 1% or 2%, or is a flat minimum dollar amount, something like $15 or more. Paying the minimum avoids the penalty fee, but interest continues to accumulate on the unpaid balance.

Consistently making only the minimum required payment on your balance can cause your debt to swell quickly. You may end up with a balance that can take years to pay off, not to mention the many dollars you will have wasted on interest payments.

The following example (see Figure 6.1) shows how long and how much money it takes to repay a credit card balance if only small monthly payments are being made on a large balance with a high interest rate. In this hypothetical situation, the borrower has a $2,000 credit card balance. The card has an annual interest rate of 21% and the borrower is not making any additional purchases with the card.

There are three payment schedules shown. In the worst case the borrower follows payment schedule "A," taking ten years (120 months) to pay off his credit card, making $40 monthly payments. During that period the borrower would have paid *$2,795 in interest fees in addition* to the original balance of $2,000.

It gets better if the borrower pays off the card at a rate of $70 a month, but it still takes over three years (40 months) and $797 in interest payments to do so.

Example – Credit Card Debt Repayment of $2,000 (21% interest rate)

Payment Schedule	Monthly Payment	Months to Pay Off Debt	Interest Paid Over the Years
A	$40	120 months	$2,795
B	$50	70 months	$1,470
C	$70	40 months	$797

FIGURE 6.1 This assumes no new charges are being made to the credit card while the balance is being paid off.

Clearly, it is not wise for an individual to build up a large credit card balance and make only small monthly payments on it. It requires a long time to pay the balance off and costs a lot of extra money in interest expense. From this example you can see why it is so important to develop the habit of fully paying off a credit card balance every single month, to not let a balance build.

If you do find yourself having to carry a balance, paying it off as quickly as possible is one of the smartest things you can do. That way you can avoid throwing your money away on useless interest payments, and the strain of a growing credit card balance affecting other areas of your life.

Grace Period

The one indulgence offered by most credit card companies is known as the monthly *grace period*. It is the interest-free period during which a cardholder is given to pay their bill.

If your credit card company offers a grace period and if you pay off your account balance every month in full before the grace period ends, there is no interest charged to your account. You have in essence been given a short-term interest-free loan every month. How wonderful!

Unfortunately, a lot of people don't do this. Instead of paying the total amount of their bill, they carryover some of the balance each month, accumulating lots of interest charges along the way and potentially creating a depressingly large credit card balance.

Fees

All credit cards have potential fees. Possible fees range from annual maintenance charges to balance transfer fees to penalty fees. *Penalty fees* are one of the most frequent charges. If your payment is late, or you exceed the borrowing limit on your account, or your last payment was returned for insufficient funds (you didn't have enough money in your checking account to pay your bill), you may be charged a penalty, perhaps something like $35. By making on-time payments, limiting your charges, and monitoring your checking account balance, penalty fees can be avoided.

In addition, because of the Credit Card Act of 2009, finance companies cannot approve card transactions that will cause a consumer's credit card account balance to exceed the account limit *unless* the consumer specifically requests that this to be permitted. This is called *opting in*. If you have not opted in and you try to purchase something that would cause you to exceed the card limit, the transaction should be refused. Avoid over-the-limit fees by not opting in.

Cash Advances

Many credit cards can be used to get a *cash advance*. A cash advance is like an instantaneous loan you receive against your credit card account. Typically a cardholder can receive a cash advance by using a credit card at an ATM and getting cash on the spot, by withdrawing cash at a bank branch office by talking with a teller, or by using one of the blank "convenience checks" that credit card companies periodically mail to cardholders.

Normally a usage fee is added, something like 3% to 5%, along with interest. There is usually no grace period before interest begins to accumulate (meaning, the finance company will start calculating interest on the balance immediately) and the interest rate is often higher than on regular card balances.

When you press the submit button at the ATM, or your cash advance check is processed, the interest starts piling up. For example, if you took out a $1,000 cash advance on your account with a 5% fee, then $50 (5% of $1,000) would be added to your account balance, and interest would begin accumulating on this total cash advance balance of $1,050 (the $1,000 original balance plus the $50 fee). If the annual interest rate were 24%, a $21 interest charge would also be added to your balance at the end of the billing period (assuming the loan hadn't been repaid yet). This gives you an even higher cash advance balance of $1,071 ($1,050 plus $21 interest). That works out to 7.1% in interest and fees for the first month! Interest continues to be charged every month the balance is outstanding.

This represents the worst of all worlds: an upfront fee, high interest on top of the fee, and no grace period before the loan balance starts building up interest charges. Using cash advances can quickly lead to a staggering credit balance.

The Payoff Schedule

One of the most informative sections now required on credit card statements is a schedule that shows the cardholder how long it will take to pay off the current balance when only the minimum required monthly payments are being made. It also shows the sum total amount of these payments, including interest. (You might ask to see this section on one of your parent's current credit card statements.) The difference between the total payments and the current balance is the interest charges that will be paid over time.

This schedule illustrates the cost to the cardholder of only making small payments on the card and letting a credit card balance roll over from month to month. Depending on the balance, the cardholder can end up paying a lot of interest and having a credit card balance that lingers for years. In addition, even though this schedule doesn't show it, the cardholder can make a bad situation worse by continuing to make purchases with the card before the balance is paid off. Piling on more debt this way, month after month, can eventually lead to a huge financial problem.

Prepaid Cards Are Not Credit Cards

What about prepaid cards? These cards are growing in popularity. Some people use them as a substitute for having a bank account, and parents sometimes like to use these cards as a convenient way to supply their children with money and also as a budgeting teaching tool.

Prepaid cards are often wrongly referred to as credit cards. They are not. Prepaid cards look a lot like credit cards, and frequently have familiar finance company logos on them. They can be used to make purchases online and in stores and some can even be used at ATMs.

There are two fundamental ways that prepaid cards and credit cards are different:

1. Unlike credit cards, prepaid cards must be loaded (money deposited into the account ahead of time) before the card can be used.

2. Prepaid card usage is not normally reported to any of the three major credit bureaus, and therefore can't help or hurt your credit history.

When you use a prepaid card you are using your own money to buy things (or the money of whoever loaded the prepaid card for you). The cards can be periodically reloaded as needed.

These cards also have fees associated with them. Some typical fees are monthly maintenance fees, reloading fees, and ATM usage fees. Different prepaid cards have different sets of fees. Anyone interested in a prepaid card should carefully investigate the related fees beforehand.

For people who don't want a credit card or don't qualify for one, a prepaid card can sometimes be a useful option. Just watch out for those fees.

Now, let's get back to credit cards…

Getting a Credit Card

First, know that whether or not to get a credit card is something you probably want to discuss with your parent. The world of credit can be a beneficial place or a nightmare, depending on how you handle it.

Some people are just not ready for a card yet. Knowing the limits of your self-control and discipline are key. It's important to be honest with yourself.

Here are some questions for you and your parent to consider when deciding whether or not you should get a credit card:

Questions to Answer When Considering Credit Cards

- Is having a credit card important for your security while away from home, in case of emergency?

- Will you be needing to rent an apartment and sign a lease in your name in the near future?

- Will you soon be responsible for maintaining a car on your own while away from home?

- Will you be applying for a permanent job soon?

- Do you see the need for a cell phone contract in your name in the near future?

Before you talk to your parent about credit cards, you might want to draw up a spending plan for yourself (see chapter 4 on spending plans for the details). Having a well thought out spending plan in hand can be reassuring to both you and your parent that you are in control of your money habits and that you are not going to go on a crazy spending spree with a new credit card.

New Credit Card Regulations

Whether or not you are eligible to get a credit card account in your name depends on your age and your employment status. Given the legislation that Congress passed in 2009, you must now be at least 21 years of age to get a credit card account solely in your name or have an "independent means of repaying any obligation arising from the proposed extension of credit" (meaning, if you are under 21 you must have a job or some other regular income that will allow you to make payments on credit card debt).

However, there are ways of sharing responsibility with an adult for an account that will give you access to a card. Read on.

Having a Co-Signer

If you don't have an independent source of income, you can still get a credit card by having an adult (someone age 21 or older, who has a verifiable independent means of income) *co-sign* on a credit card account. For most teens this would be a parent.

Asking someone to be a co-signer on your credit card account is no small matter. It means that as a co-signer they will be equally responsible for the repayment of any debt on the account, and the management of this debt will be reflected in the co-signer's credit report, as well as yours.

The co-signer shares the account with you, even if you are the only one using it. And if, for some reason, you failed to make monthly payments the finance company can come after both you and the co-signer for the money. Essentially, when you ask someone to co-sign, you are asking them to trust you with their credit history.

Being an Authorized User

Becoming an *authorized user* on your parent's card is another alternative to actually having a credit card account in your name or having a parent as a co-signer on an account. When you are an authorized user of an account, you are allowed usage of the card, but you are not legally responsible for paying off the debt on the account, the accountholder is. Of course, this means that your card activity will be reflected in the credit history of the accountholder. They are trusting you with their credit score.

Some credit card companies will include the card activity as part of the authorized user's credit history. Some companies do not. You can check with the company about their reporting policies and request that the credit card activity be included in your credit profile. This could be a good way to begin building a good credit history, assuming the payments are being made on time and that credit limits are not being over utilized.

Keeping Out of Trouble

If you do end up getting a credit card, you can do the following to manage it well:

1. Create a monthly spending plan before you get a card and stick to it after you have the card, tracking your monthly credit card purchases using your spending plan categories.

2. Always pay your monthly balance in full and before the due date.

3. Don't authorize your credit card company to permit you to make over-the-limit charges (don't opt in).

4. Avoid cash advances.

5. Set up a monthly reminder on your calendar to pay your bill on the same date every month, and make this several days before the monthly due date to be safe.

6. If you slip up and carryover a balance, do everything you can to pay it off the following month, and stop using the card until there is a zero balance.

7. Never lend your card or card number to anyone.

8. Check your account online weekly to make sure all transactions are correct and that there is no unauthorized usage (identity theft).

9. Never use your card to make tuition or room and board payments (a student loan is much more economical and flexible option).

10. Check your credit report online once a year from each credit bureau for free at *www.annualcreditreport.com*.

If You Carryover a Balance

Sometimes we make mistakes. We screw up. If you exceed your spending plan one month and cannot pay off your credit card bill, then it's time to take immediate action.

First, stop making purchases with the card. Put it away in a drawer and forget about it until you have paid off your balance (interest charges and all). Don't compound the mistake by carrying over a balance to another month. Aside from the money you will be wasting in interest, one of the worst things you can do is develop the habit of spending more than you make.

Find the money to pay off the card balance—slash your discretionary spending, decrease your monthly savings, and take on extra work to create more income. It's better to delay your goals than to build a large credit balance. In other words, do whatever you can to pay it off as soon as possible.

Perhaps you need to adjust your spending plan too. Review your projected income and spending by category and compare it with your actual income and spending. See where the differences occurred. Once you know where you strayed from your spending plan, you can decide whether this was a one-month blip or whether it will be a recurring problem, which requires you to fine-tune your plan.

Recommit to following your spending plan after you have made any desired adjustments. Once the card balance is back to zero you can begin using it again, but this time you may want to check your balance more frequently, to curb your card usage and to stay within your spending plan limits.

If you're repeatedly not able to pay off your monthly balance, this is a signal that now is probably not the time for you to have a credit card. You would be better off paying down the card balance to zero and closing the account, rather than developing some bad habits and damaging your credit history.

Credit Card Types

If you plan on getting a credit card, there are several things to understand before wading in. Credit cards types vary. Some offer cash back, while others let you earn points, which you can use later to make purchases. Some cards can only be used at particular stores, and yet others are designed to support certain charities or organizations.

Actually, a credit card may offer a combination of these features. Card types frequently overlap. Below is a discussion of the basic card types, although in reality many cards are a mixture of these.

Retail Credit Cards

If you've bought something in a store lately you may have noticed how the sales clerks sometimes ask shoppers whether they have that particular store's credit card and, if not, then would they like to apply for one on the spot and save money on their purchases.

What they're offering is a retail credit card. Many major retail establishments have their own credit card that is used for buying merchandise in their stores. The cards are usually free, have no annual fees, and some provide special discounts and other perks if you use their card when making purchases.

Reward Credit Cards

Many cards allow customers to earn rewards by making purchases with the card. Rewards can be anything from getting cash back on a percentage of card purchases, to earning points that can later be redeemed for merchandise or services.

Rewards are calculated as a percentage of the dollar amount of purchases made with the card. For example, if the reward rate is 2%, then to earn a $300 plane ticket would require that you make $15,000 worth of purchases over time on the card ($15,000 x 2% = $300). Cardholders may earn credit towards such things as airline tickets, gasoline, nights at specific hotel chains, or may be able to redeem points to acquire merchandise or other services.

There are a seemingly endless number of creative reward programs out there. Some card companies charge an annual fee and some do not. Perks are nice, but they should not be the driving force in your card selection, particularly if you won't be using the card a lot.

These cards work best for people who charge a lot on them and pay off their balance every month.

Standard Credit Cards

These are your plain vanilla credit cards that can be used most anywhere. They aren't associated with any store, charity or group, and don't provide rewards. Interest rates and fees vary from issuing company to issuing company, but may be lower because they don't offer other features.

Affinity Credit Cards

These credit cards are associated with a group or organization and will usually have the name of the organization and maybe a related picture on the card. With some cards, every time the cardholder buys something using the card, a small portion, perhaps .5% or so, of the amount charged is sent to that particular organization, often a charity or some other non-profit group.

Unless you charge a lot on the card every month, these dollars earned for charities or other organizations from your card purchases would be a relatively small amount, although with lots of consumers using the cards the total dollars can be significant.

Secured Credit Cards

For people who are trying to repair their credit history or who have a very limited credit profile, these cards may be a good starting point. With a secured card the cardholder is required to maintain a cash security deposit of a certain amount in an account linked to the credit card. The amount of the security deposit, limits how much the cardholder can charge on the card.

After a period of time, if the cardholder builds a good payment history, the finance company may allow the secured card to be transitioned to a regular credit card.

Student Credit Cards

Some finance companies offer credit cards geared towards young adults, like college students. These cards usually have a low credit limit and no annual fee. Financial companies offer them to students as a way of beginning a financial relationship with a young consumer. Sometimes they offer rewards, like cash back on certain types of purchases, and other incentives.

For young people who want to get a credit card account in their name, student credit cards are often a good way to start. The low initial credit limit and lack of annual fees can work well for beginners. Students are given enough room to work with, but, hopefully, not enough to get into serious debt trouble.

There is one drawback to note on these cards: because of the low credit limit, students need to be careful not to access too much of this limited credit. Remember that a high credit utilization ratio hurts a person's credit score, whereas a low ratio helps build a higher score.

Recap: Credit Card Management

Credit cards can be beneficial if used wisely. They can provide security in case of emergency, they can be useful where debit cards, checks, or cash just won't do, and they can be used to help build a good credit history. On the other hand, misuse of them can harm an individual's credit rating and create a huge debt burden.

Here are some things to remember about credit cards:

1. Create a spending plan before considering a credit card.

2. Understand the credit card terms in the agreement before signing up.

3. Pay card balances on time and fully every month.

4. If a balance can't be paid off in the current month, don't let it grow. Stop using the card and cut your spending to get the balance to zero as soon as possible.

5. Avoid cash advances—they are one of the quickest ways to sink deeply into debt.

6. Check your account online frequently to keep to your spending plan and to catch fraud.

7. Your parent may be willing to be a co-signer on an account with you, but remember that your actions affect their credit history.

8. Your parent may add you as an authorized user on an existing account, again know that your actions can affect your parent's credit score.

9. Credit cards are a convenience that may or may not be a good option for you at this time. There's usually no rush.

Additional Resources

✓ For a step-by-step explanation of how to read a credit card statement:

Internet search>> *site: mycreditunion.gov Understand Your Credit Card Statement*

✓ Go to *www.creditcards.com* for credit card search help and general information

✓ For more help with credit card selection:

Internet search>> *site: nerdwallet.com Best Student Credit Cards*

✓ To find debt payoff calculators:

Internet search>> *site: creditcards.com payoff calculator*

Internet search>> *site: money-zine.com debt reduction calculator*

✓ Go to *www.ftc.gov/idtheft* to learn more about identity theft and how to report it, as well as ways to protect your accounts and information

7

Making College More Affordable

A ccording to a 2013 study by the Institute for College Access & Success, seven out of ten seniors graduating from nonprofit colleges had student loan debt. The averaged debt was $28,400. Total student loan debt in the U.S. is pegged at over one trillion dollars. It's reported to be larger than either American credit card or auto loan debt. It is a serious problem. These debts will take many years to pay off, doubtless being a drag on consumer spending for years to come and influencing many life-changing decisions.

Yes, college is expensive, and getting more so every year. But there are things that you can do to lessen the cost for yourself. Obviously, you and your family want to save as much money as possible for college, easing some of the financial stress. And you can improve your chance of getting scholarships by doing such things as maintaining excellent grades and being involved in community service and other extracurricular activities. Beyond this, you can further enhance your chance of getting more financial aid by selecting schools that are generous in offering financial help to students.

Before getting into some methods of decreasing the cost of college to you and your family, let's talk briefly about the financial aid system.

How Financial Aid Works

When you begin to apply to colleges, if you want to be considered for federal financial aid, you and your parents will need to complete the *Free Application for Federal Student Aid* (FAFSA), administered by the U.S. Department of Education. The FAFSA is a document detailing your finances and your parents' income and assets, tax returns, and family situation. This information is the basis for calculating your *Expected Family Contribution* (EFC) for the coming college year.

The EFC is not necessarily what you and your family must pay, but it is what the federal government expects that you and your family can afford to pay towards the cost of your college education. This EFC number can be shockingly high and not anywhere close to what your family thinks they can afford. Schools use this estimate to assist in determining the financial aid package that they will offer you.

The complete cost for attending a given college for a year is called the *Cost of Attendance* (COA) at that particular institution. Costs are made up of college tuition, room and board, fees, and other expenses.

Cost of Attendance (COA)

The total cost of what the average college student is expected to spend per year at a given school. Costs include such things as tuition and fees, room and board, books, transportation, and personal expenses.

After you have completed and submitted the FAFSA, a *Student Aid Report* (SAR) will be sent to you and to whichever prospective schools you selected when completing the application. The SAR shows your EFC and summarizes the FAFSA data. If you file and sign your FAFSA electronically, your report should be available in five days or less after your submission.

Schools will use the SAR data to determine which federal grants, work-study, and loans you qualify for, as well as which school-based scholarships and grants they want to offer you. Once you have been accepted to a school, you will receive a financial award letter, which explains how much and what type of aid the institution is offering you.

The financial aid offer is composed of some or all of the following:

✓ Federal grants (which don't have to be repaid)

✓ School-based scholarships and grants (these also don't have to be repaid)

✓ Federal *work-study* (federally subsidized part-time jobs for college students)

✓ Student loans (these have to be repaid, they're debt)

Some private schools have additional financial aid applications that prospective students need to submit, the most common being the *CSS Profile*. Private schools use the CSS for a more thorough look at your and your parents' finances. Some of these schools may consider things that are not included in the FAFSA, such as the market value of your family's home minus any debt on the house (meaning, the home equity value) when determining aid packages. This can indicate a higher expected financial contribution than the FAFSA alone would.

Estimating Financial Aid: FAFSA4Caster

The U.S. Department of Education offers a quick federal financial aid calculator called the *FAFSA4Caster*. It provides an estimate, based on information you input, of federal aid you may qualify for.

The calculator is anonymous, does not require any identifying information. It takes about 10 minutes to complete and asks for such data as your age, income, state of residency, and your family's income, size, and asset net worth.

What you receive will be estimates by category of federal aid you may be offered, like grants, Work-Study, and student loans.

(Internet search>> *site: ed.gov FAFSA4Caster*)

Apply for financial aid as early as possible. (The FAFSA can be filed beginning October 1, 2016 for the 2017-2018 award year.) Schools often divvy up financial aid according to who applies first—the money available each year is not endless and will run out at some point. You don't want to be the last in line.

The financial aid cycle has to be repeated every year. The FAFSA and CSS are good for only one year and must be resubmitted with updated information for each year that you want to be considered for aid—even if you only qualify for federal student loans.

Generosity of Schools

Besides submitting financial aid documents, you can improve your chances of receiving more aid by applying to schools that offer more generous financial aid packages. Not all colleges have the same level of financial resources available or the willingness to part with them to lessen the financial burden for students and their families.

Some colleges are looser with their purse strings than other schools, or they have a bigger purse (endowment) to begin with. It's no secret as to which schools tend to be more giving. The statistics are available, but you will need to do a little digging.

College Board Website

The College Board's website (remember those people who bring you the wonderful SAT experience?) is a good starting point for finding data on financial aid award percentages by college, for just about any school you might be interested in.

At the College Board's website click on the "College Search" button or something similar near the top of the page. This will take you to a page where you can either search for an individual school by name or create a filtered search, using such criteria as the average SAT or ACT scores of admitted students, selectivity level of the college, location, tuition and financial aid (listed under the tab marked "Paying"), and majors offered.

For example, you could filter for schools in California that are very selective and that meet 80% or more of student financial need. This may give you a list of 25 to 30 schools to investigate. Click on any school to see detailed information about the particular institution. If you go to the "Paying" section and then click on the "Financial Aid by the Numbers" tab you'll be taken to charts, graphs, and numbers that lay out the financial aid situation at that school.

The financial aid section will show you the average indebtedness of graduating students (the average dollar amount of loans taken out by students), the average non need-based aid (meaning, not based on family and student income and assets), and average need-based scholarships and grants awarded, as well as other things. Most telling is the financial aid distribution pie chart. It shows the percentage of aid that is scholarships and grants (*gift aid*) versus loans (debt) and work.

All other things being equal, schools that provide a higher percentage of financial aid that is in the form of scholarships or grants, rather than loans and work, are more attractive. When applying to college, schools that are known to award generous financial aid packages that lean heavily on the non-loan side may be an important consideration if you're worried about being burdened with high student-loan debt when you graduate.

College Navigator Website

Another information-rich website covering the majority of colleges is the federal government's College Navigator website (*www.nces.ed.gov/collegenavigator*). At this site you can do a search by college name and receive detailed information about that school's financial aid statistics. Click on the financial aid section to see information about the number of and percentage of students receiving different categories of grants, scholarships, and student loans, and the corresponding dollar amounts.

At the bottom of the financial aid section look under the heading "All Undergraduate Students" to see the annual percentage of students receiving grants or scholarships and the average dollar amount. Then look at the annual percentage of students receiving federal student loans and the average dollar amount. You can compare these numbers between schools to see how they measure up to one another. Again, scholarships and grants are the preferred type of financial aid because you don't have to repay them.

Below the financial aid section are the useful *"Net Price"* statistics. Select the "Net Price" tab to get a rough idea of what you and your family can expect to pay per year to send you to that institution. .This section displays estimates of the average amount students and their families paid for a given year towards the total expense of attending that school, after grant and scholarship awards. The schedule is broken out by family income brackets and by year.

For example, if your family income is between $48,000 and $75,000, look under that income bracket to see what the average net price was for such a family. If it was, say, $7,000 at XYZ University for the academic year 2013-2014, then that was the average amount that a family in that income bracket paid from their own resources—whether it be in the form of student or family income, assets, or loans—for their child to attend that university.

Just because a school is a public university or college doesn't necessarily mean that it will be cheaper for you to attend compared to a private school. You first need to factor in the financial aid package. The final cost depends on how much scholarship and grant money you are offered in relation to the COA of the school. Net price estimates can be helpful when comparing schools.

Estimating Your Cost: Net Price Calculator

The net price represents an estimate of the money that you and your family will need to provide for a single academic year, whether it be from earnings, savings, or loans. In other words, the Cost of Attendance (COA) minus grants and scholarships equals the net price.

The easiest way to find the calculator is to go to the U.S. Department of Education's website (Internet search>> *site: collegecost.ed.gov net price calculator*) and type in the name of the school, or you can visit the school's website.

You will need to gather some personal financial documents, such as your and your family's recent tax returns, as source data.

You can get a more individualized picture of your family's potential financial obligation, by going to a selected school's *net price calculator*. Click the link at the bottom of the Net Price section for that institution to be taken to the school's net price calculator. Fill in specific information about your family situation, income and assets, and the calculator will provide a net price estimate based on your inputs. Just remember that these are only estimates and only for the first year of college — they are not guaranteed and can change significantly after the first year.

There is also other useful information by school in the College Navigator database, such as data on tuition and fees, enrollment demographics, average SAT and ACT scores, majors offered, diversity data, and crime statistics. School searches can also be filtered by majors and programs of interest, by state and distance from your home, by 4-year and 2-year institutions, as well as by public and private schools.

Other Ways to Minimize College Costs

Selecting schools that routinely offer a high percentage of gift aid is only one approach to improving college affordability. There are other ways to lighten the financial load. What follows are additional things to consider:

Grants

The awarding of grants is based on the financial need of the applicant and their family. Both federal and state grants are available.

There are four major federal grants:

- Federal Pell Grant – for undergraduate students with exceptional need.

- Federal Supplemental Educational Opportunity Grant (FSEOG) – like the Pell Grant, this is for low-income undergraduate students, although these grants are not available at all colleges.

- Teacher Education Assistance for College and Higher Education (TEACH) Grant – for undergraduate and graduate students studying to become elementary or secondary school teachers. It requires the recipient to work four years in high-need (low-income) schools, within eight years of program completion.

- Iraq and Afghanistan Service Grant – aid for students whose parent or guardian died in military service in Iraq or Afghanistan post 9/11.

Maximum award grants change yearly (the Pell Grant maximum was $5,730 for 2014-2015). The U.S. Department of Education's website provides information on these grants (see "Additional Resources"). Colleges use your EFC and SAR data to determine if you qualify for these grants. You should be notified of these grant awards in your financial award letter from the schools that accept you.

There may also be state grants available (usually for in-state residents who will be attending in-state schools) having their own requirements and deadlines. Some states require that other forms be completed in addition to the FAFSA, and many of these forms are due early in the year.

To find out what is offered by a given state and how and when to apply, go to the federal Department of Education website to find a directory of state programs (Internet search>> site: *ed.gov resource directory by state department of education*). Select the state you're interested in and you'll be taken to that state's landing webpage. From there select the web link under "State Higher Education Agency" to find the information you're seeking.

Once you've familiarized yourself with what's available, talk to financial aid administrators at your preferred colleges to get further assistance in understanding the process and deadlines.

Again, funds are limited, so start this process early.

Scholarships

Scholarships are another form of gift aid. There are many types available, some being for academic achievements, others for community service, and yet some are specialty awards. There are scholarships for students majoring in such things as confectionery food science or for students who are promising science fiction writers or inventors.

Many books have been written about how to get scholarship money, and there are numerous websites with useful information (see "Additional Resources").

Here are some things to consider:

- Your high school career center or guidance counselor should have information on scholarships—this is a good place to begin looking.

- The financial aid offices of your prospective schools should have information on scholarships.

- Your city's local service organizations (like Rotarians, Lions, or Soroptimists) often have scholarships.

- Your parents' work place may offer scholarships to children of employees, or one of your grandparents may have belonged to a union or some other organization that awards money.

- Your place of worship may offer scholarships.

- If you are of a certain ethnic heritage or nationality, or if you are disabled there may be award money available.

- Many states offer scholarships, check with the department of higher education for your state and the state of your preferred college or university (see "Additional Resources").

- Organizing your search process helps—keep a list of scholarships you're applying for along with items required for applications, documents you've provided, submission deadlines, when applications were submitted, and which scholarships you've won.

- Letters of recommendation may take a while to get back from your teachers or others. Making requests as early as possible is important.

- A short note of thanks to those who've helped you is always a good practice.

One thing to investigate is whether and how outside scholarships (meaning, those not offered by the college where you will be attending) will impact your financial aid package. Some schools will consider outside scholarships as fulfilling a portion of their school-based gift aid to you, and therefore may lower the amount of school-based scholarships that they offer you.

For example, if you were originally offered a $10,000 scholarship from XYZ University, and later you were awarded an outside Rotary scholarship of $2,000, the school may reduce the amount of the school-based scholarship offered to you by $2,000. The $10,000 XYZ University scholarship may be reduced to an $8,000 scholarship.

On the other hand, some colleges will calculate outside scholarships as first reducing your student loans, work-study, and summer employment contributions before lowering school-based scholarship money in the financial aid package. This is more favorable to you because it reduces your financial obligation, rather than taking away school-based scholarship money from you.

In any event, outside scholarships need to be reported to your college financial aid office and may cause your financial aid package to be refigured. Check with the school to find out how they treat outside scholarships in financial aid calculations.

Start at Community College

One option is to begin your journey in higher education at a local community college and then later transfer to a 4-year school. Going to community college for your first two years can save you a bundle in tuition and fees. And you can super-size your savings by living at home, cutting down on room and board expenses. If you use these first two years to fulfill your general education requirements, planning your courses carefully, you may be able to switch over to your state university system or a private college to finish off your last two years. No one cares where you entered college, just from which school you got your diploma.

There are specific rules concerning such things as course requirements and minimum grade point averages that have to be followed in order to transfer schools. You can contact the school you are interested in transferring to about their process and which course units they will accept from a given community college. It is also a good idea to meet regularly with a community college counselor to ensure that you stay on track with the right coursework.

Be a Dorm Resident Assistant

Keep costs down by taking a position as a dorm resident assistant (RA) sometime after your freshman year in college. RAs often receive free or discounted room and board for taking on the job. The college normally will train you to be a peer counselor to younger students. You live in the dorm with other students and guide them through the academic ups and downs and the social realities of college life. It's a big responsibility, but can be quite rewarding for someone who enjoys mentoring others.

Defer for a Year

If you're short on funds you might consider deferring college for a year after you've applied and been accepted. If you lived at home while working, this could allow you to save up more money for college. And if you have a sibling who will also be going to school in a year or two this may maximize both of your financial aid awards; financial aid offers are more generous when more than one family member is attending college concurrently because the EFC is divided between two or more schools. It's possible that deferring for a year could work in your favor in that way.

Many colleges will allow students to take what is known as a *gap year* to work or pursue volunteer service. It's best to find out in advance from the college what their policy is on gap years, and to get written permission in advance to ensure that your spot is being held. Be sure to research whether and how this will affect your financial aid award before going ahead with anything. Talk with your prospective school's financial aid office to sort this out.

Above all, make certain that you *have a concrete plan for what you will do during the gap year—a specific monetary goal, and a definite date as to when you will enroll in college.* The danger of deferring for a year is that the year stretches from one, to two, to three years or more, and college gets put off indefinitely in favor of earning money.

If you fear you lack the drive and discipline to return to school, then deferment may not be a good alternative for you. Try other avenues instead.

Nonprofit Service Work

If you are a service-minded individual, you might consider working for a nonprofit service organization for a summer or a year. AmeriCorps is one example. This national organization working in partnership with local and national nonprofit groups provides communities with services, like tutoring and mentoring disadvantaged youth, operating after-school programs, improving health care, cleaning up parks and streams, and combating illiteracy.

AmeriCorps members are offered education awards and sometimes, depending on the service, a small living stipend in exchange for hours of service. Some schools may "match" the educational awards by using scholarships or academic credit.

Check with your prospective colleges. If you want more details go to *www.nationalservice.gov/programs* for more on AmeriCorps programs.

Again, taking off a year before starting school, or any years during school, would be considered taking a gap year. And, as mentioned earlier, you should have a solid workable plan for returning to school before considering a gap year. Also, thoroughly investigate the financial aid policies of prospective schools concerning gap years and service work before making any commitments.

Military Service

You might consider the Reserve Officers' Training Corps (ROTC). Hundreds of colleges and universities across the nation have ROTC programs on campus or share a program with another nearby college or university. You can even participate in ROTC while attending Ivy League schools like Yale, Princeton, Columbia, or Harvard. Begin with the website of the school you're interested in to find out about ROTC offerings.

When you enroll in ROTC you take the normal coursework for your educational institution along with additional coursework specific to the branch of the military you are interested in—Army, Air Force, Navy, or Marines. If you meet eligibility requirements, there are ROTC scholarships which you can apply for that can meet a portion, or sometimes all, of your college tuition expenses, and may also pay for books and a monthly stipend.

Of course, in return for accepting scholarship money you will be required to serve a term in the military after graduation, such as four to eight years.

Comparing Financial Aid Offers

Once you have received acceptance letters from colleges and the related financial aid packages, you can see how the offers measure up to one another.

The College Board website (*www.bigfuture.collegeboard.org*) has a financial aid calculator for comparing awards of up to four colleges at a time. The information from your aid offers—such as tuition and fees, room and board, scholarships and grants, work-study, and loans—can be used to plug into the calculator. The calculator will summarize the financial aid offers by school and give a breakdown of gift aid, loans, and work-study as a percentage of the total financial aid offer, as well as how much money your family would need to contribute for you to attend each school.

Financial aid offers are not written in stone. If you can show that there are significant special circumstances or important facts that haven't been factored into the offer, financial aid officers may revisit the financial aid award. You and your family will likely need to prove your case, with official documents and such, as to why additional aid should be granted.

There are student loans available through the federal government, as well as parental loans. Every family situation is different. Some families will spare no expense to put their child through college and are willing to take out loans to help pay for their children's education, others families are not, and expect the student to bear any debt load. And many families fall in the middle of these two extremes.

These are very personal and individual decisions to be made by you and your family. No doubt, much discussion will be required. Loans are an obligation not to be taken lightly—the borrower is legally responsible for repaying the money along with interest payments.

You can use some of the suggested techniques in the next two sections to help you decide what loans, if any, you are willing to be responsible for. Carefully assess the numbers, the size of monthly loan payments you would have to shoulder. (The standard term for a federal student loan is 10 years.)

And, of course, all of this number-crunching and soul-searching should be done way *before* you decide to accept any school's offer.

Student Loans

According to a 2011 Pew Research Center study, the lifetime difference in earnings between someone who has a college degree and someone who doesn't is as much as $550,000 over 40 years (this is even after taking into account the expense of paying for college). College isn't cheap, but in the long run it's usually worth it in terms of increased earning power. Another positive is that on average it is easier to get a job if you have a degree than if you don't—the unemployment rate for college graduates is about half that of those without a college degree.

That said, you can also create a huge financial headache for yourself by taking out too much in student loans. Individuals sometimes don't give enough thought to what they are committing themselves to before they sign on the dotted line for a student loan. (See the next section for a discussion of possible ways to determine acceptable student loan debt amounts.)

If you are contemplating student loans to help pay for college there are two basic types: federally funded loans and private loans. Federal loans are nearly always going to be the least expensive and more flexible option. No credit check is required for undergraduate federal student loans, and while the standard repayment term is 10 years, there are also other federal repayment plans as well that allow borrowers to adjust payment amounts and terms according to their financial circumstances. You have to complete the FAFSA every year you wish to be considered for federal loans; loans are issued one year at a time and are included in your financial aid package from your college or university.

The total undergraduate borrowing limit, *subsidized* and *unsubsidized* loans combined as of 2016 is $31,000 for dependent students. There is also a yearly ceiling on borrowing. It starts lower for freshmen year and then gradually rises each year. To see the details go to the *www.studentaid.ed.gov* and type "loan limits" into the search box.

Some student borrowers wanting to go beyond these federal student loan borrowing limits may be considering private student loans in addition to federal ones. This is rarely a good idea. It's often difficult for high school seniors to know what career path they will choose down the road or what their future income will be. So, venturing into the world of private loans to borrow additional money could potentially lead to an extremely stressful financial situation once a student has to begin loan repayment.

If you find you need to use private loans to afford the college you have selected, then perhaps it's time to reevaluate the school and your financial resources. Consider this, if you had $31,000 in student loans (the maximum federal loan limit) as a graduating college senior, given 10 years to repay the loan and at the current 4.29% interest rate, you would need to pay over *$300 every month for 10 years* to repay these loans. That's quite a commitment. Now imagine if you were to add private loan payments on top of these federal loans, and you can get a sense of the financial weight of this debt.

Subsidized and Unsubsidized Federal Student Loans

Subsidized Loan – if you have a subsidized student loan, the government pays the interest on the loan for you until you graduate and pass the six-month grace period for repayment to begin. You qualify for this type of loan by meeting certain low-income requirements.

Unsubsidized Loan – you still get the same six-month grace period after graduation before you have to start repaying this type of loan, but the government will not be making interest payments on your behalf while you are still in school. Interest will begin accumulating at the time the money is disbursed (paid out) and will be calculated daily and added to the loan balance (this is called *capitalization*). Unless you start making interest payments while you are still in school, your loan balance will grow as interest accumulates. There is no low-income requirement for this type of loan.

Percentage of Income Guideline

There is no hard and fast rule as to how much debt a student can afford to take on. Some experts recommend limiting monthly loan payments to no more than 8% to 10% of the expected future gross monthly income after graduation (income before taxes and other payroll deductions). Other financial professionals say students should limit their total loan debt to their expected first year salary. These are only *suggested maximums*—hopefully, a student would be borrowing a much smaller amount, if any at all.

There is no single rule that everyone agrees on. Financial experts come up with these guidelines assuming a mythical average individual in an average situation. There's a wide range of differences that creates an average. And your life could be exceedingly unlike the average. Perhaps you have other debt already or other financial responsibilities, or maybe you're just not comfortable owing that much money and know you wouldn't handle it well. All of these things deserve careful reflection.

As an exercise, let's look at how to calculate the loan amount based on a percentage of gross monthly income. We'll use an assumed 8% of expected gross income to calculate a hypothetical maximum student loan burden.

First, you would make a future salary estimate. There is a list of websites at the end of this chapter (see "Additional Information") that can help approximate salary levels for different careers. Many students have only a vague idea of which fields interest them, so it's best to be conservative with salary estimates. (You don't want to find yourself stuck in a job someday because you took out a lot of student loans when you were younger and overestimated your future salary level.)

Second, once you have an estimated annual salary number convert it to a monthly number by dividing the annual salary by 12. And then, assuming 8% of monthly income as the maximum loan payment, take 8% of the monthly salary estimate and to get the corresponding payment amount (multiply the salary by .08).

Third, translate this monthly loan payment into the corresponding total student loan amount by using an online loan calculator. For this, you will need to input 1) the loan term (how many years to pay off the loan) 2) the interest rate on the loan, and 3) the monthly payment. In this exercise, the assumed monthly payment is the 8% of the monthly salary estimate. As of July 2015, the standard federal student loan repayment period is 10 years (120 months), and the interest rate is 4.29%. Given these inputs, and an online calculator you can estimate what the monthly loan payments convert to as a total loan obligation.

The online loan calculator at DinkyTown.net works well for this (Internet search>> *site: dinkytown.net enhanced loan calculator*). Have the calculator solve for the loan amount by selecting "loan amount" in the "calculate for:" dropdown box. The grayed-in box will show the corresponding loan amount. You can play around with the various inputs (trying out different monthly payments, interest rates, and loan terms) and see how they affect the loan amount.

The problem with this "percentage of income method" is that 1) it's difficult to know what is a reasonable percentage to use for figuring the maximum monthly loan payment (is 8% too high?); and 2) salary estimates may be very inaccurate because they depend on guesstimating career choices, geographical location, and other variables far off in the future. It's important to try alternative methods for estimating maximum student loan amounts (see the next section for one).

A knowledgeable adult could be extremely helpful in going through these exercises with you. You will want to explore all your options and related costs thoroughly before committing to any large financial obligation.

Future Budget Guideline

Another way to determine your borrowing limit is by taking a bottoms-up approach and working backwards. To do this you'll need to create a hypothetical spending plan for yourself, a best-guess budget. Your parent, or some other adult, may help you devise some of these numbers.

First, estimate your post-graduation monthly living expenses. This would include such things as rent, utilities, medical/dental costs and insurance, cell phone payments, car insurance, car maintenance, gas, food, clothing, emergency and other savings, discretionary spending, and so on. (You can find useful budget worksheets at *www.moneyandstuff.info*.)

Next, estimate your net income (income after taxes). Again, if you have some idea of the career path that you want to follow, online salary estimators can help determine annual earnings numbers (try Indeed.com, *www.indeed.com/salary*).

To convert these gross salary numbers (meaning, before taxes and other payroll deductions) into *net income* numbers (meaning, after taxes and other payroll deductions), you can use online paycheck calculators. The calculators subtract from your earnings items such as federal and state income tax, social security taxes, and Medicare taxes to get to a net income number. A useful net salary calculator can be found at Paycheck City's website (Internet search>> *site: paycheckcity.com payroll calculators*).

And finally, compare your estimated net income number with your budgeted annual expenses. Once you subtract your estimated annual spending plan number from your estimated annual net income, you have rough idea of what is the remaining money available annually for making loan payments (divide this number by 12 to get a monthly number). You can then think about how much of this available money you would be willing to commit to making monthly student loan payments over a 10-year span.

This monthly student loan payment number that you determine can then be worked backwards to calculate what this means in terms of a total student loan amount. Follow the steps discussed in the previous section, "Percentage of Income Guideline," about using an online calculator to estimate the equivalent student loan amount.

This bottoms-up exercise is designed to help you to make an educated decision about any student debt you may be considering, before accepting an offer from any school. You can use it along with the "Percentage of Income Guideline" method, or other techniques you come across, to assist you in evaluating possible student loan amounts. Again, discuss this in depth with your parents and other objective knowledgeable adults before committing to anything.

Pointers for Estimating Expenses and Income

Salary – be conservative, use lower salary estimates and avoid assuming a high-paying profession.

Hourly Wage Rate – for an hourly wage rate (this is required in some online net salary calculators) divide the expected annual income by 2,080 hours—which is a 40 hour work week times 52 weeks—to get your hourly wage rate.

Housing Expense – if you want to live in an expensive city, then factor in a higher housing expense number. Housing costs will likely be your single highest monthly expense, so be sure to use a realistic number.

Emergency Savings – estimate at least 20% of income for savings and unanticipated events.

Recap: College Affordability

1. When selecting colleges to apply to include ones that have generous financial aid policies. Pay close attention to net price estimates for schools you're interested in. Search College Board's website and the federal government's College Navigator website for data.

2. Use the EFC calculator at College Board's website - and input numbers for your and your family's finances and personal details to get an EFC estimate.

3. Search and apply for scholarships. Be creative in your research, using a variety of sources, and organize and track your progress.

4. Consider ways to lower the cost of higher education by being flexible in your thinking (see the section "Options for Minimizing College Costs" for ideas).

5. Apply for financial aid by completing the FAFSA and CSS Profile (if required). Early is usually better, as financial aid is often on a first-come, first-served basis until it runs out. State grants may have early deadlines and additional forms to complete.

6. Determine the maximum amount of student loan debt you think you can handle when you've graduated (ask your parents and other knowledgeable adults for help, and review the "Student Loan" section).

7. When you receive acceptance offers, use College Board's website to compare financial aid packages for your prospective schools. Pay close attention to any student loans listed as financial aid—the lower the student loan number the better.

8. Before committing to a school and any student loan debt, consider whether this fits with your future budget after you've graduated. If not, discuss this with your parents and the college financial aid officers to find other ways to reduce the loan portion of your financial aid or consider less costly schools.

9. Reapply for financial aid every year in order to be considered each year—even if you don't get school scholarships or grants, you still need to apply to qualify for federal student loans.

Additional Resources

✓ To find out about FAFSA and the CSS Profile go to these websites:

www.fafsa.ed.gov

http://student.collegeboard.org/css-financial-aid-profile

✓ These websites have information on college selection, costs, and student loans:

www.nces.ed.gov/collegenavigator

www.bigfuture.collegeboard.org

Internet search>> *site: consumerfinance.gov compare financial aid*

✓ To research scholarships and grants visit these websites:

Internet search>> *site: ed.gov grants and scholarships*

Internet search>> *site: collegeboard.org scholarship searches*

Internet search>> *site: ed.gov resource directory by state department of education*

Internet search>> *site: fastweb.com scholarships*

✓ Following is an informative book, written by a college student, about winning scholarships:

Confessions of a Scholarship Winner by Kristina Ellis (Worthy Publishing 2013)

✓ There are numerous financial aid and loan calculators online—here are some good ones:

Internet search>> *site: finaid.org Student Loan calculators*

Internet search>> *site: dinkytown.net enhanced calculator*

Internet search>> *site: studentloans.gov loan calculator*

✓ Current interest rates on federal student loans can be found at:

Internet search>> *site: ed.gov student loan interest rates*

✓ Visit these sites for information on salaries and for online paycheck calculators:

www.salary.com

Internet search>> *site: paycheckcity.com payroll calculators*

www.salarycalculator.org

✓ The California Career Zone website, designed for California residents, has useful budgeting information and tools that students from any state can use:

Internet search>> *site: cacareerzone.org budget*

✓ See these two books for ideas and information about scholarship and other free money for college:

Peterson's Scholarships, Grants, & Prizes 2015 (Peterson's Publishing, 2014)

Kaplan Scholarships 2014 (Kaplan and Reference Service Press, 2013)

✓ Although the following book is addressed to parents, it's full of useful suggestions about how to graduate college with little or no debt, and it's also written by a college student:

Debt-Free U by Zac Bissonnette (Portfolio/Penguin 2010)

8

What a Car Really Costs

D o you remember the scene from the movie *Spiderman* when Peter (Toby McGuire) is sitting in the car with his Uncle Ben (Cliff Robertson)? And Peter's uncle looks him in the eyes and says solemnly, "With great power comes great responsibility." Well, owning a car is kind of like that.

Someday, in the not too distant future, you are probably going to want to purchase an auto. And before you do it's important to have some idea of what buying and owning a car really requires. Many people go into car ownership with blinders on. They only see the auto, how cool it looks, fantasizing about the great trips they'll have in it, and how easy life will be now that they have wheels.

It's true, a car is a great convenience and can give you more flexibility in your life. It can be much easier than using pedal power or taking public transportation, and you may eventually need one for commuting to work or perhaps one for college. For many a car represents independence and freedom, a sign that you have reached adulthood.

But everything has a cost.

To buy a car without first knowing the real monthly expense of ownership is like buying an airplane ticket to Europe without having any idea of how long you'll be there, where you'll stay, how much your food and lodging will cost, and how you'll pay for it all. You probably wouldn't do that, so why buy a car that way?

Besides the money you pay up front to buy the car (the *down payment*), there are also many ongoing expenses: insurance premiums, annual registration fees, oil changes, tire and brake replacement, other repair costs, gasoline, and possibly loan payments (depending on whether or not you borrowed money to buy the car). Understanding what you're signing up for before you slip into the cushy driver's seat of that waxed-to-perfection driving machine, can help keep your emotions from overpowering common sense.

Let's look at the real cost of buying and owning a car.

The Purchase Price

The total price of buying a car includes not only the purchase price, but also *registration*, *license*, and *title* fees, as well as *sales tax* (in most states). All of these combined make up the final out-the-door cost.

There are several websites you can use to find sales price data on vehicles (see "Additional Resources"). You can input specific features such as paint color, interior, engine choice, navigation systems, and so on, for the year, make, and model of the car you are curious about and receive average sales price estimates. Once you have this number in hand, you can figure out the other components of the purchase price.

Car Fees and Taxes

Sales Tax or Use Tax – when a car is sold most states charge the buyer sales or use tax. It is typically calculated as a percentage of the sales price of the car.

Title and Registration Fees – the title and registration documents establish who owns the vehicle, lists the make, model, year, vehicle identification number, car license plate, and registration fees. Payment of periodic registration fees are required to renew the registration. Registration requirements and fees are set by states.

Other Fees – there are frequently additional fees tacked on to a car's sales price, like a "documentation fee" (for processing the paperwork related to the sale), "dealer prep" (for preparing the car for departure), "dealer installed accessories" (nonstandard stuff added on to the car by the dealer), or "administrative fees." Question the seller about these additional fees before agreeing to anything.

Sales tax is likely to be the largest cost in addition to the purchase price of the car. There is a base state sales tax rate, plus sometimes an additional percentage amount for county/city tax. This total sales tax percentage is then multiplied by the purchase price of the vehicle to get the dollar amount of tax required (note: there are a few states that do not have sales tax).

If you are buying a used car from an individual you may still have to pay state tax. However, it's called use tax instead of sales tax. The Department of Motor Vehicles (DMV) typically collects use tax when you register the car.

Some states have online calculators or charts to help estimate registration fees and sales tax or use tax for new and used cars, based on the purchase price and other information. You can visit your state's DMV website to see if they offer such tools.

An alternative is to use a car cost calculator, like the one at CarMax.com (Internet search>> *site: carmax.com tax title tags fees calculator*). You can get an estimate of your state sales tax, title, and registration fees for a vehicle if you provide the location and an estimated purchase price.

It really is true that the market value of a new car can decrease drastically the first year of ownership, the average is around 20%. If the purchase price is $20,000, then it will be worth approximately $4,000 less on average in 12 months. Psychologically, people automatically discount the value of something if it's used. Once the box is open or the seal is broken, it suddenly becomes less desirable, and so it is with a new car. And vehicle styles change and new features are always being added to the newest models. Cars are not usually an investment—they typically do not increase in value overtime, they decrease.

Look at your financial resources and ask yourself a question: How important is it to have a brand new car? Would a used car do just as well? Perhaps a pre-owned vehicle that has 30,000 miles or more on it already would be just fine. A used car can be significantly cheaper than a new one.

Some pre-owned vehicles sold at car dealerships have been carefully inspected and even come with warranties. Naturally, these normally cost more than cars you'll find in ads offered by individuals, but the extra expense may be worth the assurance of a fit vehicle.

If the used car you are thinking of buying is not certified with a warranty, or if you don't know the credibility of the owner, paying for a mechanic to do a pre-purchase inspection before buying is a good idea. Besides telling you the overall health of the car, a mechanic can also alert you to any major maintenance issues that are on the horizon.

Vehicle Identification Number (VIN)

All cars produced since the early eighties have a standardized 17-character VIN inscribed somewhere on the vehicle. The VIN can usually be found on a small metal plate displayed on the car's dashboard where it meets the windshield, visible from outside the vehicle on the driver's side.

Car buyers can use the VIN to trace a car's registration, accident, and recall history. Law enforcement use them to trace missing or stolen vehicles.

You can also do a little detective work yourself by going to CarFax.com or AutoCheck.com. At these sites you can get a used car's vehicle history report, if you know the car's *Vehicle Identification Number* (VIN). To get a detailed report expect to pay around $30 or $40 (note: car dealerships sometimes offer consumers free reports on used vehicles in their inventory). The report gives information on such things as major accidents reported and structural damage, flood damage, recall and warranty information, as well as recent reported odometer readings.

Be aware that this information is not necessarily all inclusive. There is a lag time between when repair work is done and it is reported, and there may be unreported accidents and repairs done "off the book." Many auto buying experts still recommend having an independent mechanic check a used car over.

Now, let's look at the monthly expenses of car ownership, item by item.

Auto Loans

Cars aren't cheap and are getting more expensive every year as new safety features, specialty electronics, computers, back-up cameras, and all sorts of other bells and whistles are added. Unless you have financial help from a relative or friend, you may not have enough money to pay the total cost of a car when you need one.

At some point in the future you may be considering an auto loan. If you decide to finance (borrow) part of the purchase price, there are some basics things to understand.

There are three key variables in auto financing:

1. The *principal* amount of the loan (the amount of money you are borrowing).

2. The *interest rate* on the loan (the fee you are charged for borrowing the money).

3. The *term* of the loan (the length of time you will be borrowing the money).

The monthly loan payments are a combination of interest and principal payments. Naturally, the more money you pay up front, the less you'll need to borrow (meaning, the lower the principal amount). And the less borrowed, the lower your monthly payments will be.

The interest rate and term of the loan will also affect the size of your monthly payments. Figure 8.1 illustrates the impact that different interest rates have on monthly loan payments and Figure 8.2 shows the effect that shorter and longer loan terms have on monthly loan payments.

The Impact of Interest Rates on Monthly Payments
(3-year loan of $10,000)

FICO Score	Hypothetical Interest Rate	Monthly Payments	Total Payments over 3 years
Excellent – 720 or better	3%	$290.81	$10,469
Good – around 650	9%	$318.00	$11,448
Poor – in the 500s	15%	$346.65	$12,479

FIGURE 8.1   Hypothetical interest rates as of late 2015.

First, we see in Figure 8.1 that the interest rate is influenced by the borrower's credit score, in this case the FICO score (see the "Understanding How Credit Scores Work" chapter for more on FICO scores). A higher FICO score indicates to the lender that the individual is a better credit risk (meaning, more likely to make payments on time and in full). This is why people with higher scores usually get offered lower interest rates. And the lower the interest rate, the lower the corresponding monthly loan payments.

In Figure 8.1 a person with excellent credit is hypothetically offered a 3% interest rate and the person with poor credit gets a 15% interest rate. The excellent-credit individual pays $2,010 less over three years than the borrower with poor credit ($10,469 versus $12,479 in total payments). You can see that having a better credit score can potentially save a consumer thousands of dollars in interest.

The Impact of Loan Terms on Total Payments
($10,000 Loan at 9% interest)

Year	3-Year Loan		7-Year Loan	
	Monthly Payments	Annual Total	Monthly Payments	Annual Total
1	$318.00	$3,816	$160.89	$1,931
2	318.00	3,816	160.89	1,931
3	318.00	3,816	160.89	1,931
4	---	---	160.89	1,931
5	---	---	160.89	1,931
6	---	---	160.89	1,931
7	---	---	160.89	1,931
Total		$11,448		$13,517

FIGURE 8.2 The difference in the totals is interest.

Look at Figure 8.2 to see how changing the loan term impacts the size of total loan payments. In this example the loan amount is $10,000 and the interest rate is 9%. For a three-year loan the borrower pays a total of $11,448, this includes repayment of the original $10,000 plus $1,448 of interest. For a seven-year term, total payments amount to $13,517.

Notice that although the monthly car payment for the seven-year loan is actually $157 smaller than for the three-year loan ($318 versus $161 in monthly payments), the amount of interest paid over the seven-year period versus the three-year period is actually $2,069 more ($1,448 versus $3,517 in interest). It is a tradeoff—to lower monthly payments the borrower has to pay the lender off over a longer time period, which means paying out more in interest over the years.

Those extra dollars of interest go into the lender's pocket, never to be seen again by the consumer. Even though the seven-year loan is more "affordable," in terms of the size of the monthly loan payments, the borrower is actually paying out more money overall, an extra $2,069, over the seven years.

If you are thinking of a long-term car loan, be aware of what could happen if you chose to sell the vehicle before the loan is fully repaid: It's possible that the car's market value (current sales price) could be less than the remaining balance owed on the loan at the time you want to sell it. (This is called being *upside down* on your loan.)

How is it that the current value of your vehicle could be less than the outstanding balance on the loan (money still owed the lender)?

Well, the typical auto loan is a *level-payment loan*, which means that the payments are the same every month throughout the life of the loan. However, only a portion of every monthly payment goes towards repaying the principal amount (the money originally borrowed), and the rest goes towards interest charges. Over the course of the loan, the share of the monthly payments that is being applied to principal versus interest changes.

The slice of each monthly payment that goes towards interest is larger in the beginning and decreases over time. And the reverse is true with the principal portion of the monthly payments. The principal is paid off less quickly in the early years of the loan and faster towards the end.

This could mean that if you had a seven-year loan on your car and you wanted to sell it early, say, after four years, you might find yourself in a situation where your car's market value is less than what you still owe the bank on the loan. If you sold the car, you wouldn't receive enough money to pay off the loan—you'd still need to come up with more money to pay the bank for the remaining loan balance.

Not a good situation.

Taking on a lengthy car loan can be a financial drain. If you can't afford car payments unless you stretch the loan out over seven years, you might want to take a step back and reassess the situation. Seven years, 84 months, is a long time to be making car payments!

A short-term loan, such as three years, with a large down payment may be the better option. Sometimes, given a stable employment situation, you might consider a five-year loan. And there is always the alternative of waiting to buy the car until you can save up for a larger down payment and are able to take out a smaller loan with a shorter term.

Estimating Car Payments

To estimate the potential loan payments for a vehicle you will need to know how much money you will be borrowing and at what interest rate and for how long. The amount to be financed (borrowed) is the difference between the total purchase price (including taxes and fees) of the vehicle and the down payment you plan to make. You can make a better estimate of the interest rate you're likely to receive if you know roughly what your credit score is. Your credit score will be a key factor in the interest rate on your loan. Having a better credit score will usually get you a lower rate.

To see your official FICO credit score you may have to purchase it. (Actually, there is no single score that all businesses use to evaluate consumers, there are several types of scores, each for different purposes.) You can purchase your standard FICO score at myfico.com from one of the three credit bureaus (Experian, TransUnion, or Equifax). You don't need to buy all three, any one should be fine—the scores should be similar.

Currently, it costs around $20 to get your FICO score from a credit bureau (bypass advertisements for credit monitoring services by using the following search: Internet search>> *site: myfico.com one-time credit score*). However, some large banks and credit card companies offer their customers free access to their credit score through the FICO Score Open Access program.

Alternatively, you can get a free credit score by going to sites like *www.CreditKarma.com* or *www.Credit.com*. While these sites don't provide official FICO credit scores (at this writing, Credit Karma provides the Vantage 3.0 credit score based on a 300 to 850 point scoring range), these companies supply credit scores that can give you a good idea of the strength of your FICO score.

Once you have a number to work with, you can use it to determine possible interest rates for auto loans and the corresponding monthly payments. If you go to the myFICO website you can find a calculator that displays a table of average interest rates and monthly payments by FICO credit score groupings. You supply the loan type (term) and loan amount and the calculator fills in the table according to your inputs. The results can also be filtered by state. You can experiment by using different loan terms and principal amounts to see how the monthly loan payment is affected (Internet search>> *site: myfico.com loan savings calculator*).

Variable-Rate Car Loans

There are some lenders who offer variable-rate car loans to consumers, where the interest rate changes over time. The starting interest rate is usually lower than for a comparable fixed-rate loan, but the interest rate fluctuates after an initial time period. The interest rate will be calculated based on a key, widely published interest rate, like the prime rate, plus additional percentage rate points.

The variable rate may eventually end up being higher than the comparable fix rate that the consumer could have originally received. The maximum and minimum allowable increase or decrease (the cap) in the variable interest rate depends on the loan contract, as does the frequency with which the interest rate can be adjusted.

Budgeting for a variable rate loan can be difficult because the interest rate may change from year to year, which means that the loan payments can be hard to predict.

Zero-Percent Financing

What about all those zero-percent financing deals that zip across the TV screen periodically? With zero-percent financing, the borrower only repays the principal (the amount borrowed)—there are no interest charges as long as the loan payments are made on time for the duration of the term.

Sometimes they can be a good deal, and sometimes not, depending on the circumstances. Here are five things to consider:

1. These deals usually apply to only a limited pool of automobiles.

2. If zero-percent financing *and* cash rebates (discounted pricing) on a vehicle are available, the buyer usually has to make a choice of one or the other.

3. Sometimes a cash rebate together with a low interest rate credit union or bank loan may cost you less than zero-percent financing in the long run.

4. If you make a payment late, the zero-percent rate may be cancelled and replaced with a high interest rate.

5. To get a zero-percent finance offer the borrower may need to have a very good or higher credit rating.

Auto Insurance Costs

If you accidentally lost your sweater, left it on the grass at the park, would it be a financial struggle to replace? Would you be devastated for days on end? Probably not.

Now imagine you recently bought your first car, a late-model Honda Civic, $14,000 worth of car. You wash it lovingly every week, take pictures of it for your friends to see, and tell everyone about it.

One night your car is parked on the street in front of your house and wham! Someone plows right into it in the middle of the night. You hear the sickening crunch of metal and run out to check on your baby only to see the unthinkable—your shiny new car is wrecked, it looks like Thor has been beating on it with his hammer. And on top of this, the perpetrators didn't even have the decency to stick around to take the blame. You only have $500 in your rainy-day fund, body work is expensive. This could set you back $3,000 or more. Then you remember, "Ah, I have insurance!" And you sigh with relief.

States require the owner of a car to carry some minimum amount of insurance. When some unfortunate event occurs where your car is damaged or stolen, or someone else is injured or their car is damaged, and your auto was involved, then insurance comes into play. You notify your insurance company about the event, in other words *file a claim*. Your insurance company can then get the ball rolling to handle the situation.

Basic Components of Auto Insurance Coverage

Bodily Injury and Property Damage Liability – covers expenses related to the other person(s) or other property(s) involved, when you, the driver, are at fault for causing an accident. Covers costs related to injury, sickness, death, and property damage.

Personal Injury Protection – covers medical expenses for you, the driver, and your passengers following an accident.

Collision – covers related expenses when your car collides with another car or object.

Comprehensive – if your car is damaged or destroyed by fire, windstorm, flood, vandalism, etc., this covers the expense. Car theft is also covered here.

Uninsured/Underinsured Motorist Coverage – covers expenses for damages caused by the other driver who is uninsured or underinsured.

(Note: coverages are subject to various dollar limits.)

The way it works is that you pay a periodic fee to the insurance company in exchange for insurance coverage. This fee is called a *premium* (which could be paid either monthly, quarterly, semi-annually, or annually). The premium is not the same for everybody. Insurance companies are very good at determining the probability that you will file a claim, what sort of claim, and how much it will cost them. They have unbelievable amounts of data that computers and personnel are diligently working with to provide these predictions.

One factor influencing your premium rate is your *deductible*. Depending on the circumstances of an accident or other insurance event, your insurance company requires that you bear some of the expense for the mishap, this is called your deductible. It's a way of ensuring that you have some "skin in the game," so to speak. That is, you have an interest in *not* getting into accidents because you may have to pay some minimum amount up front before your insurance company pays for anything.

Here are some things that insurance companies may take into consideration when deciding what premium to charge you:

- The year, make, and model of the car you're insuring.

- Where you live, your zip code.

- How many miles you drive the car annually.

- The size of your deductibles.

- Your age and sex.

- Your grade-point average, if you're a student.

While many of these elements can't be changed easily, you can maintain a good grade point average, choose a larger deductible (more on this later), and you can select a car that doesn't require high insurance premiums.

You may not have thought about it, but there can be a big difference in cost between insuring, say, an Audi A8 versus a Honda Accord. (The Audi will cost more to insure, all other things being equal) Why? There can be lot of reasons for the difference in insurance cost. Some factors that may influence the premium are the cost to replace the vehicle if it is destroyed or stolen, the average theft rates of such vehicles, the typical cost of repair work, and the average safety ratings of the car. These all affect the premium that insurance companies will charge the owner of a vehicle.

Also, the more you agree to pay out-of-pocket for an accident, the deductible, the lower the monthly premium your insurance company will charge you. All other things being equal, you'll save on premium payments if you choose a $500 deductible over a $250 one.

If you do choose a higher deductible, it's a good idea to have the deductible amount set aside somewhere (for example, $500), in case you do have an accident and must pay up. (Talk to an insurance company representative to find out what the actual difference would be in your situation if you chose a higher deductible.)

Insurance Company's Ratings

When choosing an insurance company don't let price be the only factor. The reputation of the company is important. You want to do business with a company that will follow through swiftly on their commitment to you if you get into an accident and file a claim—you don't want to be waiting around weeks to get your car repaired and for the claim to be resolved.

You can find consumer ratings research of insurance companies at http://www.jdpower.com/ratings/industry/insurance.

One other thing to remember about premiums is that if you have an accident and you are at fault and file a claim, your insurance company may increase your premium in the future. The more accident-prone you are in their eyes, the more insurance companies will charge you in premiums. You may become classified as a higher-risk individual. Some insurance companies are more forgiving than others when it comes to adjusting premiums after claims have been filed.

Compare the insurance premiums of two or three different companies using the same deductible assumptions and coverage amounts, for the car models you're considering. Make a worksheet, like the one in Figure 8.3, to evaluate your choices. You might call or visit the website of your parent's insurance company and two or three well-rated companies to get quotes for comparison. The companies will likely ask you to choose deductible limits, provide information about yourself, such as age and sex, employment status, address, miles driven annually and for what purpose, and details concerning the vehicle you want to buy.

Insurance Quotes Worksheet

	Company 1	Company 2	Company 3
Car A	$	$	$
Car B	$	$	$
Car C	$	$	$

FIGURE 8.3

DMV Fees

Car owners have to pay state registration and license fees. These fees go towards paying state Department of Motor Vehicles (DMV) and highway patrol costs, as well as providing property tax payments to local government. Some state DMVs have online calculators you can use to estimate fees, or you can call the DMV office for help in estimating annual fees.

Once you have an estimate, divide this number by twelve to get the monthly expense:

__Monthly DMV Expense__ = Annual Registration & License Fee ÷ 12

(Note: as your car ages, these fees normally decrease, but for the sake of simplicity and to be conservative assume that DMV fees remain constant from year to year.)

Gasoline

Fuel costs will be one of the top monthly car ownership expenses. The fewer miles driven and the better the car's fuel economy, the lower this recurring expense will be. The miles per gallon (mpg) for virtually any car can be found by going online to *www.fueleconomy.gov*. There are three numbers for fuel economy. One is for city driving, one is for highway driving, and one is a combined average of the two. Choose the number that matches the type of driving you expect to do most. If your driving will be relatively evenly blended, then use the combined number.

Predict how many miles a month you will be driving and divide your mileage by the vehicle mpg. This will be your estimated monthly gallons of gas purchased. Take that number and multiply it by the current cost of gas and you have your monthly fuel expense.

For example if the fuel economy for your potential car is 24 mpg and you expect to be driving 600 miles a month, then divide 600 by 24 to get 25 gallons as your monthly gas usage. If gas costs $4.00 a gallon, then you would expect to spend around $100 a month on gas (25 gallons x $4.00 per gallon).

Here's a summary of the calculations:

Monthly Gallons of Gas = *Estimated Monthly Mileage ÷ mpg*

Monthly Gas Expense = *Monthly Gallons of Gas x Price per Gallon*

Maintenance and Repair Costs

Cars need oil changes, new tires every few thousand miles, new brakes now and then, tire rotation, new transmission fluid, filters replaced periodically, and so on. These are car maintenance costs, and they go hand in hand with car ownership. One way to estimate these expenses is to use an online car ownership cost calculator.

Kelley Blue Book has a helpful calculator that will provide 5-year total cost estimates for various car models (see "Additional Resources"). The calculator provides a lot of information. It offers not only estimates of maintenance costs, but also of fuel costs, insurance premiums, registration fees, loan payments, and *depreciation* (the decrease in the market value of a car over time). The calculations are based on several assumptions, such as the annual car mileage, down payment made, and the auto loan interest rate. The calculator allows you to adjust the standard 15,000 annual miles driven by substituting a different number. You can also change the financing costs by selecting your own interest rate and down payment amount or set financing to zero by checking the "I don't plan to finance" box.

The year-by-year details of the 5-year cost estimate is visible once you click on the "Yearly Breakdown" tab. Here you will find the costs by category and by year, such as yearly fuel expense, insurance premiums, and maintenance. If your potential car is relatively new, you may wish to use the maintenance and repair estimates given by the calculator.

Some of the other cost estimates may or may not be that relevant to your situation, such as depreciation. Depreciation represents the yearly decrease in the value of the vehicle and is not an actual cash outlay each year. You wouldn't need to include it as an annual budgeted car expense. (However, depreciation will be a consideration if you need to sell the car to buy another vehicle.) And insurance quotes gotten from insurance companies will probably be more accurate than what the calculator will give you. In short, feel free to manipulate these category dollar estimates so that they apply to your situation, using some of the methods discussed in this chapter.

Online car cost calculators can serve as a starting point for any late model vehicle you are considering, but if you are looking at a car that is, say, five years or older, or one with high mileage, these tools are much less helpful.

Getting information from a knowledgeable auto mechanic can help you create reasonable maintenance and repair costs. A good mechanic should be able to give you an approximate idea of annual car servicing costs for your chosen vehicle. If you are worried that a mechanic won't provide you with this information, explain to him or her that you are not only looking for cost estimates, but also for somewhere to regularly service your future car. That may help.

Service employees at car dealerships that maintain and repair the make and model of vehicle you're interested in, may also be able to give you rough estimates. And finally, your parents may be able to shed some light on car maintenance and repair costs by discussing with you their experience with their cars over the years.

Whatever the annual costs you assume, divide them by 12 to get a monthly maintenance and repair expense estimate.

Monthly Maintenance & Repair Expense = *Annual Maintenance & Repair Costs ÷ 12*

Car Longevity

If you regularly service your vehicle, following the maintenance schedule recommended by the manufacturer, your car can last many years. In the early years of a car's life the yearly cash expenditures usually decrease each year.

Why? Your auto loan payments, if any, will be zero after a few years, your insurance premiums will fall as the car ages, and your DMV fees should also decrease. Of course, maintenance and repair costs will begin rising at some point, which will offset some of these savings. But it can take many years before you reach that point.

You can get your money's worth out of your vehicle by maintaining it well and keeping it for a long time.

Buffer of 5%

Factoring in a buffer for unplanned expenses is also a good budgeting practice. Start with 5 % or so. This will help take care of any inaccuracies in your estimates and unanticipated things, like gas price hikes, bridge tolls, parking tickets (let's hope not), and other things that weren't factored in. Give yourself a little wiggle room for error.

Here's how you would calculate a 5 % buffer:

Buffer = *Total Expenses x .05*

Putting It All Together

You can use the worksheet in Figure 8.4 to total your monthly expenses. If you are using numbers from an online calculator that outputs annual costs, divide them by 12 to get monthly numbers.

This worksheet ignores car depreciation value. In terms of budgeting for your monthly car expense, depreciation isn't something you'll be paying out every month. That said, the annual depreciation of a vehicle is something to keep in mind when selecting a car because in the future you may want to sell it and use the money to help purchase another vehicle or for some other purpose.

Monthly Expense Worksheet

Description	Amount
Loan Payments	$
Insurance Premiums	$
DMV Fees	$
Gasoline	$
Maintenance & Repairs	$
Total	$
Buffer (approx. 5%)	$
Grand Total	$

FIGURE 8.4

Hopefully, your monthly car expense estimate fits into your spending plan. If not, you can look for a less expensive vehicle to purchase and maintain, or find ways to adjust your monthly spending and income, or delay the purchase until you save more money, or do a combination of these things.

Recap: Estimating Car Costs

1. Research the total purchase price of your potential car, including sales tax, registration, license, and title.

2. Estimate monthly car payments using online calculators if you plan to finance some of the cost (having an estimate of your credit score can help make your calculations more accurate).

3. Contact insurance companies for auto insurance quotes (consider higher deductibles if you have enough money saved to cover them).

4. Contact your DMV to estimate yearly registration fees.

5. Estimate your yearly mileage and calculate your monthly gasoline expense.

6. Use resources online and talk to car service departments and mechanics to estimate maintenance and repair costs.

7. Plug in all your monthly expense estimates and total them. Then add in a 5 % buffer to get a grand total monthly car expense.

8. See if this estimated auto expense will fit into your monthly budget.

9. If the monthly car expense is too great, consider a less expensive vehicle that is cheaper to drive, insure, and maintain, or postpone the purchase until you can

save more money. You also might look for areas in your current spending plan where you are willing to make sacrifices.

10. Once you purchase a car, get your vehicle serviced regularly, keep it in good working condition, and hold onto it for many years, to get the most value out of it.

Additional Resources

- ✓ For car assessment and pricing, the following websites provide useful information:

    www.kbb.com

    www.truecar.com

    www.edmunds.com

    www.carsdirect.com

    www.fueleconomy.gov

    www.carfax.com

- ✓ The My FICO website has a "Loan Savings Calculator" for estimating interest rates and loan payments based on credit scores:

    Internet search>> *site: myfico.com loan savings calculator*

- ✓ Bankrate.com has several good auto loan calculators:

    Internet search>> *site: bankrate.com auto loan calculators*

- ✓ To estimate vehicle title, registration, tax, and other fees by state, go to CarMax.com:

    Internet search>> *site: carmax.com tax title tags fees calculator*

- ✓ Edmund's has a very good article on new car fees:

    Internet search>> *site: edmunds.com new car fees*

✓ When estimating annual maintenance and repair costs, these two websites are very useful:

Internet search>> *site: kbb.com total cost of ownership*

Internet search >> *site: aaa.com "your driving costs"*

✓ Visit J.D. Power's website to find which auto insurance companies have the best ratings:

http://www.jdpower.com/ratings/industry/insurance

9

Saving Early for Retirement

 ep, here you are just starting out working at the local sandwich shop after school or delivering the evening paper, and now you're being asked to think about saving for retirement. Why bring this up now? You've got another 45 to 50 years until retirement, right? Well, you currently have an asset in abundance that your parents can never have again: *lots of time before retirement*. At this point in your life, when it comes to putting away money for retirement, time is your most valuable asset.

If you asked a middle-aged person what's the one thing they wish they had done differently with their finances, many people would say, "To have started saving for retirement earlier." You can't depend on *Social Security* (our country's retirement and disability income assistance program) to take care of all of your retirement income needs. Social Security will become less and less generous over time. In the future, you will likely have to be older to start receiving it and have to pay more taxes on it than retirees do today. It's just a matter of math—the gap is widening between the number of workers paying into the system and the growing number of people getting payouts from the system (retirees).

Social Security

The original Social Security Act of 1935 was signed into law by Franklin Roosevelt. Originally Social Security was designed to pay retirement benefits only. It has since been amended several times and now includes disability and survivor benefits.

In terms of retirement benefits, Social Security provides monthly retirement income for persons 62 years or older. The monthly payout you receive at retirement is determined, in part, by how much you have paid into the system each year via payroll taxes, as well as the age at which you decide to start receiving payouts.

The rules change periodically, such as the payroll tax percentage applied to your paycheck, the age when you can start drawing benefits and the amount, and how much of the payouts are subject to income tax. And the rules will likely be very different when you retire than they are today.

Yet another reason to begin saving for retirement is that the lifetime pensions workers used to receive after being employed by the same company for twenty or more years—steady monthly retirement checks for life—are becoming as rare as hen's teeth. The truth is that people today need to start investing early in retirement accounts so that they can generate a sizeable amount of money to draw on during retirement.

Many full-time employees are aided in saving for retirement by the convenience of an employer-sponsored retirement account, such as a 401(k) plan at work, or some other type of plan. Some employers will even match employee contributions up to a given limit (meaning, the employer contributes the same amount to the employee's retirement account, as the employee contributes to the account). Employees may be able to set aside additional money on their own in an *individual retirement account* (IRA).

There are several kinds of IRAs permitted by the federal government. They are designed to encourage people to prepare for retirement. IRAs lessen the impact of income taxes on money placed in the accounts, and left there to grow can potentially provide significant funds for retirees.

Compounding Over Decades

Your parents probably envy the oceans of time that you likely have to save for retirement right now. If you start saving early in life and invest your retirement money well, these savings can grow to an impressive amount by the time you're ready to tap into them, decades in the future.

When you invest money and then reinvest the resulting income and do this over and over again, you are *compounding* your investments. The value of your original investment can grow surprisingly large given enough time if your money is continually reinvested — this is the power of compounding.

Let's look at an example…

Think back to elementary school or middle school when a math teacher might have asked a student a simple question: "If someone offered you the choice of $1 million today or all of the money in an account that has doubled in value each day for 30 days, starting with only a single penny, which would you prefer?"

Well, you may remember the answer. The account that started with just a penny will be worth much more in 30 days than $1 million. In fact, it will total a little over $5 million at the end of a month because the money is compounding, increasing in value, at a *rate of return* of 100% a day. This rate of return represents the increase in value of the account from one time period to the next. In this case the time period is one day.

The money in the account doubles every day. Day 1 starts with one cent, by day 2 that has doubled to two cents...by day 10 it's worth $5.12...by day 20 it's up to $5,242.88...and at the end of 30 days the account holds a whopping $5,368,709!

This is an extreme example of the power of compounding — it's impossible to find any investment that increases in value by 100% every day! But it still works incredibly well at much lower compounding rates.

You have the advantage of being able to invest your savings over a very long stretch of time because it will probably be decades before you retire. It may be hard to imagine where you'll be when you're in your 60s, but by then you'd surely be glad to have a nice stash of money and to not have to depend solely on Social Security.

Look at the following example in Figure 9.1 to see the advantage of starting to set aside and invest retirement money earlier rather than later. The table shows the growth of $10,000 invested today at an assumed rate of return of 6% compounded at the end of every year (meaning, the 6% increase in the value of the account balance occurs at the end of every year—in reality, compounding usually happens more frequently). The table shows the growth of this sum for four different durations.

Not surprisingly, money invested for a longer period grows to a larger amount, but what is eye-opening is the difference in size that starting just 10 years sooner can make in the end value (future value) of the investment. In this example, invest $10,000 today and it grows to $102,857 in 40 years, but wait just 10 years to start investing and the future value is almost cut in half to $57,435.

The future value is much smaller because the money has had 10 years less time to compound. And if 30 years have passed before the $10,000 is invested, the end sum is much smaller, $17,908.

Starting early gives you a huge advantage.

Table of Future Values of $10,000 Invested

Start Date	Amount Invested	Years Invested	Annual Rate of Return	Future Value of Investment 40 Years from Today
Today	$10,000	40 years	6%	$102,857
Wait 10 Years	$10,000	30 years	6%	$57,435
Wait 20 Years	$10,000	20 years	6%	$32,071
Wait 30 Years	$10,000	10 years	6%	$17,908

FIGURE 9.1 The investment value is compounded at year end.

Still not convinced? Let's try some bigger numbers. Imagine that you are age 22, have recently graduated from college and are working fulltime. At the beginning of every year you put $5,000 into your retirement account. The money is invested in stocks and bonds (more about this later), and assume again that the account earns 6% annually. Just like clockwork, you do this for 40 years. How much money will you have in your retirement account at the end of four decades?

Your account value would be worth *$820,238.*

What if you keep putting off beginning? You wait 10 year, 20 years, or 30 years to start. Look at the following table for the answers.

Table of Future Value of $5,000 Deposited Annually into a Retirement Account

Start Date	Number of Years $5,000 Deposits Are Made	Annual Rate of Return	Total Amount of Deposits	Future Value of Retirement Account in 40 years
Today	40 years	6%	$200,000	$820,238
Wait 10 years	30 years	6%	$150,000	$419,008
Wait 20 years	20 years	6%	$100,000	$194,964
Wait 30 years	10 years	6%	$50,000	$69,858

FIGURE 9.2 The investment value is compounded at year end.

Waiting just 10 years to start will cut the future retirement account value almost in half to $419,008. If you are really late in starting, and wait 30 years to begin, you'll only have $69,858, less than one tenth of what you would have had if you had started right after college.

And an even greater expansion of your retirement savings is possible if you are consistently increasing the amount you are adding to the retirement account as your paychecks grow over the years. Regular investing and reinvesting of your money can allow you to build up a significant sum by the time you are ready to stop working.

Before discussing different ways you can invest your money, let's talk about retirement accounts and one in particular that often works well for young people.

Roth IRAs

America's tax laws allow for many different types of retirement plans, permitting individuals to save money in what are called *tax-advantaged* accounts. With a tax-advantaged account the saver is provided with a means of delaying or eliminating income tax on retirement savings. Allowing tax reductions on these retirement accounts is one method the government uses to encourage workers to save.

Your income level, employment status, and other factors determine which retirement plans you can participate in. Many employers offer retirement plans to their employees. One of the most common plans is called a 401(k) retirement plan. Employer-sponsored retirement plans typically allow employees to delay paying income taxes on a portion of employee earnings. The employee has part of his or her wages deposited into a retirement account opened in his or her name, and then uses the money to purchase investments offered through the plan. These savings will be taxed when the employee withdraws the money after reaching retirement age.

There are other types of retirement accounts that individuals can open on their own. Maybe you've heard of one type called *Roth IRAs*. People whose income is sufficiently low enough to be taxed at the lowest rates (meaning, they are in the lower income tax brackets) may benefit the most from having a Roth IRA. Many young people that are working part-time or have just started their first full-time job fall into this category.

A saver contributes *after-tax* earnings into a Roth IRA (meaning, earnings that have already been subject to income tax). The saver can periodically make contributions into the account, invest the money inside of the account, and let the investments grow tax-free until he or she decides to make withdrawals upon reaching the required retirement age. Withdrawals meeting the IRS qualification rules for Roth IRAs are tax-free (these are called *qualified withdrawals*).

This is a favorable situation for individuals who are in a lower tax bracket today but expect to be in a higher tax bracket at retirement, which applies to many younger people. For example, say you make $6,000 in earned income this year, open a Roth IRA and deposit $2,000 into the account. Because of your low earnings level, you might not owe any income tax for the year. And if you invest your $2,000 and it eventually grows to, say, $20,000 in 40 years, you can withdraw this money tax-free starting at age 59 and ½ .

How much money can you put into a Roth IRA each year?

You can contribute to your Roth IRA only as much as your reported earned income is for a given year. (The IRS also sets maximum earned income limits, according to filing status, which determines which taxpayers can make contributions.) For example, if you have a part-time job and your employer reported to the IRS that your earned income was $1,200 during the year, then that is the most that you can put into the account for that year.

There is also an annual maximum for Roth IRA contributions. For the year 2015, the maximum amount of contributions a person can make is $5,500 ($6,500 if you're 50 or older), and the contribution maximum begins phasing out once certain earned income levels are reached. The limits and rules can change every year.

Following are some Roth IRA basics for 2015, but check *www.IRS.gov* for the latest and complete rules:

2015 Roth IRAs

✓ Contributions cannot exceed your reported earned income (investment income is <u>not</u> earned income)

✓ The 2015 contribution maximum is $5,500 ($6,500 if you're age 50 or older)

✓ To make contributions your modified adjusted gross income (MAGI) must be less than $131,000 if your filing status is Single, and the contribution maximum begins phasing out once your MAGI hits $116,000 (see IRS Publication 590-A for the definition of MAGI)

✓ Only contributions (<u>not</u> the increase in investment earnings) may be withdrawn before retirement age without penalty

✓ Withdrawals from your Roth IRA (both contributions and investment earnings) that are made after you reach age 59 and ½ and once you've met the 5-year-holding-period requirement, are tax-free if you meet all other IRS requirements

✓ Under some special circumstances (for example, if you become totally and permanently disabled or you are buying a first home) you may be able to make limited early withdrawals free from penalties and tax if you meet all IRS requirements

(Note: different limits and rules apply for a designated Roth IRA within an employer-sponsored retirement plan.)

What if you withdraw Roth IRA money before retirement?

One often mentioned feature of a Roth IRA is that contributions made (this excludes any investment returns) to the account can be withdrawn without penalty before the IRS-required retirement age is reached. While this is true, doing so can seriously diminish the final value of your retirement account.

Once you remove money from your Roth IRA, there is no catch-up provision for the following year. Meaning, you are not allowed to contribute additional dollars in future years to make up for what you withdrew from your account in earlier years.

Money removed from your Roth IRA means fewer investment dollars that you can have compounding towards retirement. Withdrawing money from your Roth IRA before retirement should be avoided.

If you are under 18, can you open a Roth IRA?

If you are under the age of 18, you will typically need an adult, normally a parent or guardian, to open a custodial Roth IRA for you. With a custodial account the money in the account belongs to you, but your parent has the responsibility of maintaining and investing the account on your behalf. Together you can decide how to invest the money. When you reach, what is known as, the "age of majority" (age 18 in most the states), the custodianship ends and you control the account.

Can someone else give you money to deposit?

Yes, the money you deposit can be a gift from someone else, for instance a relative. But, you still can't contribute more than your reported earned income for that year.

When can you make deposits?

Once you have opened an account you can make contributions anytime during the year and by April 15th of the following year.

For example, you can make a deposit to your Roth IRA on April 15th of 2016 for income you earned in 2015.

Where can you open a Roth IRA?

You can open an account at many financial firms, such as a banks, credit unions, mutual fund companies (for example, Fidelity or Vanguard), or brokerage firms (for example, Charles Schwab or E-Trade). You may be able to open a Roth IRA at the bank where you currently have an account, or you might choose a more flexible option, such as a mutual fund company or brokerage firm, where there is likely to be a greater and more diverse choice of investments.

There is no limit to the number of Roth IRA accounts you can have as long as the sum total of your yearly contributions to these accounts don't exceed the IRS limits. However, most people prefer to keep things simple—when you have only one or two accounts it is easier to keep track of your retirement investments and keep fees to a minimum.

Investing

Opening a retirement account is only the first step. Next you'll, no doubt, want to decide how to invest the money that you've deposited into the account so that it can grow. There is a vast amount of information available about how to invest money. Your choices are wide ranging—stocks, bonds, mutual funds, exchange-traded funds, commodities, options, futures, and so on.

At this stage, as a new investor, it's probably best to start simple. To paraphrase superstar investor Warren Buffett, "Never invest in anything you don't understand."

Let's briefly discuss some basics.

Investment Returns

In the real world no one earns a steady rate of return year in and year out. The 6% rate of return used earlier when discussing compounding is not a given. There is no guaranteed rate of return. This chapter uses 6% because it is probably a reasonable average return given the historical long-term performance of stocks and bonds.

When your money is invested in the *securities* markets (meaning, stocks, bonds, and other investment instruments) the return can vary considerably from year to year. This *volatility* could mean that one year your investments earn 20% and the next year lose 15%. It all depends on how the money is invested and the movements of the various securities markets. But even though the returns on stocks and bonds fluctuate up and down in the short-term, the long-term trend has historically been upwards.

No one can tell you exactly what the markets will do in the future (and if someone claims they can predict it, don't believe them). But you can look at past history over long periods of time for different types of securities to get a sense of what may occur in the future. And that's a good starting place when estimating investment returns.

Stocks

At your age, because you have such a long investment period ahead of you before retirement, arguably one of the best places to invest your long-term money is in *stocks*, also known as *equities*.

When you invest in stocks you are essentially buying a piece of a company. Each "piece" is represented by a share of stock. If you buy one share of Apple Incorporated stock, then you own a small portion of that company.

Companies wanting to raise large amounts of cash to run and grow their business often issue shares of stock. Investors who believe that the company has the potential to make a lot of money will buy these shares, hoping that one day they will be able to sell the shares for much more than they paid for them originally.

Each share has value, and that value fluctuates from moment to moment based on what someone else is willing to pay to own a piece of that company. Many companies also pay *cash dividends*. A cash dividend is a periodic payment made to company shareholders for each share of stock held. Dividends come from the company's earnings and are usually paid quarterly.

Stock Exchanges

The buying and selling of stocks is carried out in various marketplaces called *stock exchanges*. An exchange can be a physical place where stocks are traded, electronic trading places, or a combination of these. America's two major stock exchanges are the New York Stock Exchange (NYSE) and the National Association of Securities Dealers Automated Quotations (NASDAQ).

Investing your money in the stock of only one company can be extremely risky. There are many unknowns that can affect the value of a company — management decisions, the price of raw materials, new regulations, competition, technological innovations, natural disasters, and so on.

Instead of buying shares in just one company, investors often seek to limit the risk of their *portfolio* (collection of investments) losing money by holding shares in several different companies operating in a wide array of industries and areas of service. This way, no single or handful of stocks can overly impact the value of a portfolio.

Diversifying investments within an *asset class* (investment type), equities in this case, is a commonly recommended investment strategy to reduce risk. By spreading money among various stock types, the impact of the change in value that any given stock has on a portfolio is limited. This *diversification* of stock holdings can help to smooth out the fluctuations in the value of a portfolio over long periods of time. But it takes more than just a few stocks to significantly reduce risk. (Later in this chapter is a discussion of some effective ways to diversify investments.)

It is also helpful for investors to spread their money between different types of asset classes. Below is a discussion of another major asset class.

Bonds

Bonds are another type of common investment security. A company or government entity can raise needed money by selling bonds to investors. The money is borrowed from investors, to be repaid at a later date.

A bond is a promise to repay borrowed money by a given date to the bondholder and to provide interest as compensation for the time period the money is borrowed. The bond agreement spells out the intervals and interest payments to be made to the bondholder. For example, if you buy a bond of the Disney Corporation for $1,000 that has a *maturity date* (the end date by when the borrowed money must be repaid) of January 1, 2040, with semi-annual interest payments of $25, then you, as the bondholder, will receive $25 from the Disney Corporation every six months as long as you own the bond and the bond has not reached the maturity date. When the bond matures, if you still own the bond you will receive the $1,000 originally borrowed.

Of course, if the Disney Corporation goes bankrupt before 2040, then you may not receive the $1,000, and you may not receive all of the interest payments either. That's one of the risks you take.

Governments, national and municipal, also issue bonds. Some countries are more financially solid than others (U.S. bonds are considered by many as the safest). Just like in the case of equities, when investing in bonds, investors should diversify among several different types and from a variety of sources in order to reduce the risk of losing money and to smooth out investment returns. One of the easiest and least expensive ways for the average investor to diversify, both stock and bond investments, is by buying shares in *mutual funds*.

Mutual Funds

When you buy shares of a mutual fund, you are buying part of a pool of securities, rather than the actual securities themselves. Each mutual fund is set up for specific objectives. Some may be designed to track the movements of company stocks in the healthcare industry, others funds might concentrate on the bonds of Latin American countries, and yet others funds seek to mirror the entire U.S. stock market. There are many choices.

A mutual fund's share price fluctuates daily. It is priced once a day after the markets have closed, and reflects the end-of-day market value of the investments that the fund holds.

Often, several mutual funds are administered by a single financial company. The mutual fund company keeps track of shareholder accounts, fund expenses, provides customer support, issues account statements, and takes care of other business functions. Each mutual fund has managers responsible for investing the money for the shareholders.

When evaluating mutual funds the *expense ratio* of the fund is an important element. The expense ratio is a percentage fee that is deducted from shareholders' assets, the assets under management in the fund. This fee is used to pay for the fund's operating expenses, the cost of running the fund, including compensation paid to the fund's managers.

Expense Ratio

A mutual fund's expenses divided by the value of total assets being managed, equals that fund's expense ratio. Expenses include such things as compensation paid to fund managers, administration fees for support staff, and operating costs.

Funds with low expense ratios have less money removed from shareholders' assets, which means that more of shareholders' resources are generating investment returns. All other things being equal, funds with low expense ratios are preferred.

You can find a fund's expense ratio by going to websites like *www.Morningstar.com* and searching for the fund by name or ticker symbol and looking under "expenses."

There will always be expenses related to running a mutual fund and most of these expenses will be paid for by the shareholders. The size of the expense ratio can vary greatly from one fund to another. However, just because a fund has a higher expense ratio does not mean that it is a better fund. It's best to seek out funds that keep their expense ratios low, because lower fees mean that more of your money is being invested in stocks, bonds, and other investments instruments, rather than paying for expenses.

Think of it this way, if you invest $1,000 in a fund with a 2% annual expense ratio, then $20 will be taken out over a year's time to pay for the administration of that fund, whereas if the expense ratio is only .5% then only $5 will be deducted as an expense fee, and the rest of your money remains invested.

If you invest regularly in a mutual fund and over a long period of time, the negative impact of a fund having a high expense ratio takes on greater importance. Over decades these fees can cost you thousands of dollars, money that could have been working to increase your account value. All other things being equal, you want funds with lower expense ratios.

While every mutual fund company charges an expense fee to cover their costs, there is sometimes another type of fee that shareholders pay. They are called *load* fees.

A load is a sales charge collected from the shareholders of a fund and is stated as a percentage of the fund's assets under management. It is a fee that financial companies use to pay commissions to financial professionals for promoting and marketing mutual funds to investors. These fees go by different names, such as front-end loads, back-end loads, or level loads, but they all have the same result of reducing shareholders' assets. These fees have nothing to do with improving the performance of a fund. They are just an extra expense that the fund shareholders bear. There are plenty of excellent mutual funds to choose from that do not charge a load.

Load versus No-Load Mutual Funds

Load mutual funds charge shareholders an extra fee (load) on assets. For example, a front-end load is a fee charged when an investor initially buys shares. These fees are typically used to pay commissions to financial representatives who sell investors shares of the fund.

No-load mutual funds do not charge these extra sales and marketing fees. There are many good no-load mutual funds to choose from, and information on them is widely available. Avoid investing in mutual funds that charge load fees.

A fund's *prospectus* spells out all fund fees. This document not only details the costs related to investing in the fund, but also discusses the fund's past investment returns, objectives, management's investment strategy, and other vital information. Every fund has a prospectus, and it should be available at the company's website. Reviewing the fund prospectus is an important step to take before buying shares in a fund.

Fund Prospectus

A fund prospectus is a document that provides important information about a fund's investment objectives and focus, expenses and fees, past performance, investment risks, fund managers, and other relevant information. It's a good practice for potential investors to read through the prospectus before investing in a fund. The prospectus can be found at the fund company's website.

There are thousands of no-load mutual funds available. Some provide more diversification than others. Investors can diversify their investments by buying shares of mutual funds that track a broad-based *index*, such as the *S&P 500 index* or the *Wilshire 5000 index*. An index is a numerical means of valuing a group of securities representing a particular market segment. In the case of the S&P 500 index, the index focuses on the stocks of 500 leading U.S. companies. And all together the price movements of these companies are considered to approximate the movements of the U.S. stock market.

Index mutual funds will frequently have the name of the index they track somewhere in the title of the fund, or may name the segment of the market that they represent (for example, "Total Stock Market"). But the only way to really know what the fund invests in is to do a little research, such as by reading the fund's prospectus or independent investment news sites, like *www.morningstar.com*, that provide insights and data on various funds and securities.

Indexes

An index is a numerical means of valuing a particular market segment represented by a group of securities. The index value is calculated using the prices of these securities, and it fluctuates as the security prices move. In this way, the index "tracks" a given market segment.

Some indexes are narrow in scope while others are very broad. For example, a very limited index is one that concentrates on the auto industry, tracking the stocks of a relatively small number of companies that manufacture and sell vehicles as well as businesses selling related parts and services. The S&P 500 index is considered a broad-based index. It focuses on 500 stocks of leading U.S. companies in leading industries (companies like Apple and Costco).

Exchange Traded Funds (ETFs)

ETFs are another investment category. They are similar to mutual funds, as they are also based on a pool of invested assets into which individuals can buy. However, ETF shares trade moment to moment on stock exchanges instead of being priced and traded at the end of the day like mutual fund shares.

To trade in ETF shares the investor typically pays a commission (fee) each time he or she buys or sells shares, just like when trading stocks. Individuals that prefer to make small and frequent investments may find this less than ideal.

Investors also need to be cautious about how they buy or sell shares during the trading day because of occasional significant security price swings during the course of the day. ETF investors can protect themselves from trading at extreme prices by using *limit orders* when either buying or selling ETF shares. A limit order allows an investor to determine the price conditions that must be met before shares are either bought or sold. The trade will only be completed if the price falls within the "limits" that the investor has set.

Given the added complexity and commissions involved with ETF trades, less experienced investors may instead wish to begin with low-cost broad-based index mutual funds. If you want more information on ETF investing strategies, do the following web search: Internet search>> *site: nasdaq.com best practices for ETF trading*.

Target-Date Mutual Funds

Even when you restrict your choices to only low-cost broad-based index mutual funds, there are still hundreds to choose from. This can be a bit overwhelming.

One simplifying solution is to invest in a special subset of mutual funds called *target-date mutual funds*, sometimes referred to as "lifecycle," "age-based," or "asset-allocation" funds. These funds are designed to take the guesswork out of investment decisions. They may be a good alternative for people who are new to the world of investing and have limited time to learn.

A target-date fund maintains a particular *asset allocation*, a mix of different asset classes within the fund. For example, a fund might currently have an allocation of 65% of assets invested in U.S. stocks, 15% in foreign stocks and 20% in bonds, totaling 100% altogether. This mix of assets represents the fund's asset allocation. Each fund's strategy is discussed in the fund prospectus.

Asset Allocation

The relative proportion of different assets classes held within a collection of investments is called the asset allocation. For example, the asset allocation of a target-date mutual fund might be 50% invested in equities (stocks), 40% in bonds, and 10% in cash.

A target-date mutual fund is often a fund consisting of other mutual funds, essentially a "fund of funds." A target-date fund may be invested in two or more mutual funds, often broad-based index types. Each fund is managed for a targeted investor retirement date. The number of years between the target date and the present date determines how aggressively or conservatively the fund is invested. (A more aggressively invested fund usually means a higher percentage of stock versus bond investments.)

Normally, there is a four digit number in the fund's name, along with the word "Target" or "Retirement," to identify it as a target-date fund. The number in the title corresponds to the projected investor retirement year.

Let's say that an investor is 18 years old and expects to retire at age 65, which means that he or she would retire 47 years from today. The individual might look for a target-date fund close to year 2063—today's date, year 2016, plus 47 years. Two funds that meet this requirement are the T. Rowe Price Retirement 2060 Fund (TRTFX) and Vanguard Target Retirement 2060 Fund (VTTSX). The letters in parenthesis are the *ticker symbols* (fund identifiers). Target-date funds are usually created in increments of five or ten years, for example, 2040, 2045, 2050, and so on.

As of March 31, 2015, the Vanguard 2060 Fund would have had the following asset allocation: approximately 62% of fund assets invested in a total index stock fund, 10% in total bond index funds, and 28% in an international total stock index fund (62% + 10% + 28% = 100%). A different target-date fund may have a different percentage mix of investments, based on the strategy for that particular fund. Some funds are more aggressive, some funds less so. The fund strategy can be found in the fund prospectus.

To maintain a desired asset allocation for a given target-date fund, the investment managers will regularly buy and sell securities to maintain targeted percentages. This is called *rebalancing*. Adjustments are required periodically to maintain the relative size of the different asset classes within a fund because security market values fluctuate constantly. Target-date funds are convenient because they automatically do the rebalancing for you.

In addition to rebalancing the portfolio, fund managers will shift the asset allocation percentages toward a more conservative stance as the target date approaches—generally, decreasing the percentage invested in stocks and increasing the percentage invested in bonds. This gradual intentional shifting of a fund's asset allocation to more stable investments is known as the fund's *glide path*, and it is spelled out in the fund's prospectus.

Why change the asset allocation over time?

Well, as people get closer to retirement they normally want to be more conservative with their investments, as they have less time to recover from any big drops in the value of their retirement savings. And bond markets tend to be less volatile than stock markets (meaning, the value of bonds don't bounce around as extremely as the value of stocks do). This is one of the reasons that target-date funds will shift more assets away from stocks and into bonds and cash as the fund's target date approaches.

Of course there is a tradeoff—with lower risk comes lower returns. As the target-date fund ages, investors should expect lower returns but with more stability in value.

Glide Path

The glide path is the strategy for shifting asset allocation percentages in a target-date fund towards a more conservative mix as the target date approaches. Typically this means decreasing the amount invested in equities and increasing the amount invested in bonds and cash as the projected retirement date nears.

If you are a do-it-yourself kind of person, you can create your own retirement portfolio by putting together a "basket" of mutual funds. You can decide on asset allocation percentages that fit your needs and maintain them annually by rebalancing your portfolio. And you can gradually shift these percentages to make them more conservative as you near retirement—in essence, create your own glide path. (See "Additional Resources" at the end of this chapter for more information on investing.)

However, you may not want to take on this challenge yet. Investing in a target-date mutual fund is an easy entry point to investing. You can always take a more hands-on approach later by selling the target-date shares and creating a self-directed retirement savings investment portfolio.

Mutual Fund Ticker Symbols

Every mutual fund has a ticker symbol for easy reference. The ones for mutual funds usually end in "X", which immediately signals that it is a mutual fund and not a company stock ticker symbol or some other type of security. For instance, Vanguard Target Retirement 2060 Fund goes by the ticker VTTSX. When you type these letters into a search engine you will get a list of websites with information about the fund.

Finding a Target-Date Fund

Three of the most well know mutual fund families that offer a variety of target-date funds are Fidelity, T. Rowe Price, and Vanguard (Roth IRAs can be opened at any of these companies). You can find information and recommendations on specific target-date funds by searching online for mutual fund reviews and suggestions in the content of respected financial publications and trustworthy personal finance websites (see "Additional Resources" for some suggestions). As with any mutual fund, you want to choose funds that have low expense ratios.

Typically, a Roth IRA applicant will need an initial deposit of anywhere from $500 to $3,000 to open an account. Many companies don't charge a *maintenance fee* (a monthly or annual charge) for a Roth IRA as long as you keep your account value above a certain dollar amount. There are also companies that will waive the initial deposit requirement if you set up a minimum monthly automatic deposit into your Roth IRA from your checking account. (As of this writing, T. Rowe Price and Fidelity have such programs.)

If you don't have much money available to open an account, but have regular income from a job, automatic deposit may be a good option. Most companies require transfer minimums of around $100 per month. When your account value has built up to the required initial deposit amount, you can cancel the automatic deposit.

When you have selected the companies you want to investigate, you can go directly to company websites and read about their account rules, fees, and mutual fund offerings. Sometimes it's helpful to talk on the phone or chat online with a company representative. Here are some important questions you might ask (the website should list a phone number for customer support):

Questions to Ask a Financial Company

- Does the firm offer custodial IRAs for investors under age 18 and what forms are required to open one?

- How much money is needed to open an account?

- Can the initial required deposit be waived if I participate in an automatic investment program?

- Are there account maintenance fees, and if so how much?

- Can I qualify for a fee waiver by maintaining a minimum balance?

- Are target-date funds offered and for what retirement dates?

- How do these funds rank in performance in comparison to similar target-date funds?

- What are the expense ratios and other fees associated with the funds, and is there a minimum amount required to invest in each fund?

- How much are account closing and transfer fees, if I decide to move my money?

Don't be shy about asking questions. Answering people's questions and helping individuals with account openings and maintenance is customer support's function. It's your money that you are considering depositing with the organization—you have every right to understand the details of how everything works.

Keep in mind that your ultimate choice of where to open an account is not a contract until death—you can always switch your account to another company if you find out later that it isn't a good fit for you. The single most important thing to do is to get started saving for retirement early in life, and take advantage of the magic of compounding over many, many years. You can always change your fund selections, asset allocations, and investment account locations later. Don't let these decisions keep you from beginning. Just start somewhere.

Recap: Starting a Retirement Account

1. Talk with your parent about opening a custodial Roth IRA on your behalf if you are under age 18.

2. Research financial companies where you can open such an account. Look for companies that offer low-cost, well-run target-date funds and low-cost broad-based index mutual funds.

3. Open the account (a custodial account with your parent if needed), deposit either the initial required contribution amount or sign up for automatic deposit.

4. Make sure your total annual contributions do not exceed your annual earned income and the annual contribution limits allowed.

5. Access your account (or, if a custodial account, have your parent do it) and invest your Roth IRA money in a target-date mutual fund that is appropriate for your expected retirement age, or in low-cost broad-based index mutual funds.

6. Review your mutual funds every year or two to see if their returns and expenses still compare favorably with similar funds. (You always have the option of moving your savings elsewhere.)

7. Make regular contributions to your Roth IRA.

8. Maximize your retirement savings by avoiding withdrawing any contributions from your Roth IRA.

Additional Resources

✓ Here are some good websites and blogs with useful information about mutual funds and investing:

Internet search>> *site: sec.gov investor info mutual funds*

Internet search>> *site: sec.gov investing and saving*

www.morningstar.com (type a mutual fund ticker symbol into the website's search box to get details on a fund)

www.money.cnn.com

www.kiplinger.com

www.getrichslowly.org

www.cashmoneylife.com

✓ For more on diversification go to these websites:

www.sec.gov/investor/pubs/assetallocation.htm

www.fidelity.com/viewpoints/guide-to-diversification

✓ *Common Sense on Mutual Funds* by John C. Bogle (Wiley, 2010) is a classic on index mutual fund investing, well worth reading for any investor.

✓ *All About Asset Allocation* by Richard A. Ferri (McGraw-Hill, 2010) for more on allocation investment strategies.

✓ Here's a beginning list of mutual fund companies to consider:

Charles Schwab

Fidelity

T. Rowe Price

Vanguard

•

✓ For current IRS rules on Roth IRAs:

Internet search>> *site: irs.gov Roth IRA rules*

✓ For more information on how ETFs work and how to invest in them:

Internet search>> *site: nasdaq.com best practices for ETF trading*

Internet search>> *site: sec.gov bulletin exchange-traded funds*

Conclusion

C ongratulations! If you've read this far, you've taken an important step on the path to financial wisdom. Now is the time to get serious about your money. With the knowledge provided in this book you can build a strong foundation for good financial planning, and you can potentially avoid many of the financial headaches some adults face today (think excessive debt, low credit scores, and insufficient retirement savings).

There is no magic to personal finance. Like most things, when you break it down into individual steps, it isn't so complex. And the more knowledge you possess, the more confident you can be in talking about money matters with others, whether it be employers, financial aid officers, insurance brokers, or investment professionals. I encourage you to get an even better understanding of the topics covered in this book by following up with the "Additional Resources" at the end of each chapter. The more you know, the better your decision making can be. It's important to always be educating yourself about your personal finances.

Beyond this, remember that some of the people in your life may be some of your best resources. Parents, guardians, teachers, and other knowledgeable adults may provide valuable help and advice—we all need a hand sometimes. Of course, getting advice from others doesn't mean that you hand the responsibility for your finances off to someone else. No one has a greater stake in things working out in your best interest than you do, so always be deeply involved.

As you go forward remember that simplicity and consistency are your two best friends. By keeping things simple you avoid hurdles to getting started and you make maintaining a plan easier, inspiring confidence in your ability to manage things. And with consistency you will soon see results from your actions, whether it's getting a job, building a good credit score, or growing a retirement account.

Here are ten key points to keep in mind:

Ten Personal Finance Points to Remember

1. Get comfortable with the world of banking—find a safe, accessible, and inexpensive place to keep your money. Frequently monitor your bank accounts to track spending and to safeguard against identity fraud.

2. Success in finding a job isn't an accident—when opportunity knocks you have to be ready with a well-planned resume, good personal presentation, and people contacts.

3. Taxes go hand in hand with income, so seek to minimize taxes—make sure your withholdings are correct, understand your W-2, and file a tax return when required.

4. Plan your spending—get in the habit of following a monthly spending plan, no matter how simple, and always save money for your future and for unanticipated emergencies.

5. Build and protect a good credit history—handle credit cards and other debt responsibly. A good credit score can save you thousands of dollar in interest payments over your lifetime and can help with employment, renting, and insurance.

6. Credit cards can be a useful tool if used carefully. Consider credit cards to be like a one-month loan—always pay your bill on time and in full every month. And monitor your account frequently to control spending and fraud.

7. Minimize the expense of college—plan ahead for ways to decrease the cost and don't take on more student loans than your future-self can handle.

8. The purchase price of a car is only the beginning—estimate the total monthly upkeep expense of an auto before buying, and see if it fits into your spending plan.

9. Saving for retirement is a lot easier if you start early—time is your greatest asset, so take advantage of it. Consider starting a Roth IRA and contributing to it regularly.

10. Personal financial planning is an ongoing evolving process—be curious, seek out new information, and keep your plans relevant to your changing life circumstances.

Every person's situation is different. Customize your plans so that they work for you. This book is a great place to begin your personal financial planning journey, but don't stop here it's only the start of your adventure.

I wish you success!

Glossary

asset allocation—the division of investments into different asset classes or categories in order to achieve various investment goals. The allocations are usually expressed as percentages, with the sum of all percentages equaling 100 percent.

asset class—a grouping of assets with similar features and financial behavioral characteristics. Three primary asset classes are stocks, bonds, and cash.

ATM—automated teller machine.

ATM/debit cards—a card, often referred to just as an "ATM card," that is linked to the cardholder's bank account. It allows the user to withdraw cash from the cardholder's account at an ATM or by visiting a bank teller. The card can also be used as a debit card to make purchases at most locations where credit cards are accepted. The money is deducted directly from the person's bank account at the time of sale.

ATM fee reimbursement—the refund of ATM fees incurred by an individual when using ATMs that are not part of the person's bank or credit union network.

ATM shared networks—a banding together of ATMs owned by several banks or credit unions. These financial institutions have an agreement allowing their customers to use ATMs within the shared network, normally fee-free.

authorized user—an individual who is not the owner of a credit card account, but who has been authorized by the account owner to use the account. The account owner is responsible for all debt incurred on the account, including the credit card usage by the authorized user.

bonds—a type of debt security representing the legal obligation of a borrower to repay borrowed money, on or before a specific date and to provide interest payments to the bondholder as compensation. A bond may have several owners over its lifetime.

capitalization—the periodic adding of unpaid accumulated interest to an existing loan balance.

cash advance from a credit card—money borrowed against a credit card account by the accountholder. Typically money is borrowed by using a credit card at an ATM or by using a cash advance check provided by the finance company. Interest charges usually begin to accumulate immediately. There is normally a usage fee as well as interest.

cash dividend—a percentage of company earnings paid out to stock shareholders on a regular basis, usually quarterly. Not all stocks have dividends.

compounding—the process of reinvesting earning on top of earnings again and again over a period of time. An example of compounding is when money is invested in mutual fund shares, and then all of the periodic earnings on shares are reinvested in more shares, and the return on these new shares are also then reinvested, and this process is done repeatedly.

credit bureau—an agency that gathers and maintains data about individual consumer credit related activities, which are summarized in a person's credit report. The three major credit bureaus are TransUnion, Equifax, and Experian.

Credit Card Act of 2009—a congressional law designed to strengthen consumer credit safeguards. One provision of the law requires that a person must be at least 21 years of age or have an "independent means of repaying any obligation" in order to independently open a credit card account.

credit card agreement—a document detailing the terms and conditions of a credit card account, such as due dates, grace periods, and penalty policies.

credit card interest—the interest charged for an unpaid balance on a credit card account. It is calculated by applying a given percentage rate against the outstanding balance on the account. Interest charges are added to the balance to create a new outstanding balance for the following billing period.

credit history—the documented credit-related activity of a consumer. Credit histories are maintained by credit bureaus.

credit limit—the maximum amount of debt that a credit card issuer authorizes the card holder to have at any given time on a credit card account.

credit report—a report detailing the credit activity of a given individual. Credit reports are maintained and distributed by credit bureaus.

credit score—a numerical representation of a person's credit management behavior. The higher the score the better. (The best possible FICO credit score is 850.) The score is derived using information from an individual's credit report.

credit unions (CUs)—not-for-profit financial institutions that function similar to banks. CUs are known for focusing on personal service and community lending. They frequently pay higher interest rates on savings deposits and often have fewer fees than commercial banks. To use CU services you must be a member; memberships are organized around specific groups, such as persons of a particular geographic region or employees of a given organization.

CSS/Financial Aid Profile—a financial aid application that some private schools require, in addition to the FAFSA, to help determine how much financial aid to offer a prospective or returning college student. The information asked for from the student and the student's family provides more detail than the FAFSA.

custodial account—a financial account set up for a minor, by a custodian (normally the minor's parent or guardian). The custodian manages the account for the minor until the minor reaches the "age of majority" (age 18 in most states), at which time the former minor takes control of the account.

debt—the amount of money owed by one party to another party. The amount of debt increases when interest and fees are added to the original borrowed amount.

debt (credit) utilization ratio—the percentage of available credit being used. It is determined by dividing the total debt outstanding by the amount of credit available.

deductible—an insurance term that refers to money that a policyholder must pay out-of-pocket on a covered loss (meaning, it is covered by the insurance policy), before the insurance company will make payments on the insurance claim.

direct deposit—having your paycheck, or some other type of regular payment owed to you, deposited directly into your bank account or some other type of financial account, instead of being paid by cash or check.

discretionary spending—money that is available for use after your financial obligations and saving requirements have been met.

diversification—the investment strategy of seeking to reduce portfolio risk and volatility by simultaneously holding a wide range of assets of different types and classes.

down payment—the money paid up front to purchase something, with the remainder being financed (borrowed money). A down payment is often used when buying expensive items like a car or home.

equities—another name for stocks (shares issued by companies). Company shares are bought and sold on stock exchanges.

estimated tax payments—are used by taxpayers to satisfy the IRS requirement that taxes be paid as income is earned. Taxpayers with fluctuating monthly income who do not have employer withholdings, such as self-employed individuals, or those who need to make additional tax payments beyond their paycheck withholdings, may need to make estimated tax payments (see IRS *Form 1040-ES*). Payments are made directly to the IRS and typically divided up into four installments, due by the 15th of April, June, September, and January.

exchange traded fund (ETF) — an investment pool of assets in which investors can buy shares. The shares trade throughout the day on stock exchanges and are bought and sold like stocks, through a broker or in a brokerage account. Fees are typically paid when shares are bought or sold.

exempt (from withholding) — when an individual's earnings are such that no withholding for income tax is required. The IRS has specific rules as to when a person's earning qualify as "exempt." It is claimed using Form W-4.

Expected Family Contribution (EFC) — a dollar amount that a student and the student's family are expected to pay from their own resources for the student to attend a year of college. It is based on the federal government's calculations using information supplied in the FAFSA.

expense ratio — the percentage applied to all assets invested in a mutual fund for the payment of fund expenses, such as compensation paid to portfolio managers and administration costs. These expenses are paid out of shareholder assets, reducing shareholder return on investments.

Fair Isacc Corporation (FICO) — a company that devised and maintains the FICO credit scoring system, the most widely used credit system for gauging the credit behavior of consumers.

Federal Depository Insurance Corporation (FDIC) — an independent agency of the federal government that monitors banks and insures depositors' money in each FDIC insured bank for up to $250,000 per depositor. The FDIC was created in 1933 as a response to numerous bank failures during the 1920s and early 1930s.

Federal Reserve (the Fed)—the central bank of the United States. The Fed seeks to maintain a healthy and stable U.S. economy, keep unemployment rates low, keep inflation under control, monitor and regulate banking institutions, and protect consumer credit rights.

filing status—an IRS designation that categorizes a taxpayer according to given factors and is used to determine which IRS income tax rules apply to the taxpayer. The filing status impacts how much tax is owed by the individual.

Free Application for Federal Student Aid (FAFSA)—an application to be completed by prospective and current college students and their families in order to be considered for federal aid (federal loans, grants, and work-study).

gift aid—financial aid that does not have to be repaid, usually scholarships and grants.

glide path—the gradual shifting of a target-date fund's asset allocation over time as the targeted retirement date nears. Typically, the equities (stocks) percentage is decreased and the bonds and cash percentages are increased over time.

grace period—the interest-free period during which a credit accountholder is given to pay their bill.

index—an investment term referring to a grouping of stocks, bonds, or other securities, designed to represent a particular market segment. For instance, the Wilshire 5000 index is designed to track the entire U.S. stock market.

Individual Retirement Account (IRA)—a retirement account that individuals can set up at financial institutions, permitting the accountholder to save money for retirement while postponing or decreasing tax payments on some or all of the assets in the account.

insurance claim—a formal request made by a claimant to the claimant's insurance company for payment of a covered loss.

load mutual funds and no-load mutual funds—mutual funds that charge a fee (load) to the shareholder when shares are bought or when shares are sold are called load mutual funds. A no-load mutual fund has no such extra charge.

limit order—a means of specifying certain price conditions that must be met before securities are either bought or sold.

maintenance fee—a periodic fee charged to customers for maintaining an account at a financial institution.

maturity date—the end date of a bond. Meaning, the date by which the principal amount borrowed is due to the bondholder. For example, if a bond originally issued on January 1, 1996 for $1,000, has a maturity date of January 1, 2016, then the $1,000 is payable to the bondholder of record on January 1, 2016.

Medicare—the federal government's medical insurance program, primarily for citizens 65 and older who have paid Medicare taxes for a given period of time. Medicare taxes, which are normally withheld from worker earnings, are mandatory for nearly all working Americans.

minimum wage—the minimum hourly wage rate an employer is normally required to pay employees per federal and state government laws. Different states have different minimum wages, and if the state wage rate is higher than the federal one, the state minimum one applies.

mortgage—a legal agreement between a borrower and a lender that allows the borrower to buy real estate, such as a house, using the lender's money and to repay the loan over a period of years. The real estate is used as collateral (security) for the borrowed money.

mutual fund—a large pool of investments that is professionally managed for the benefit of the shareholders of the pool. It can be an effective way for individuals to diversify their investments among several areas, such as different companies, industries, countries, and asset classes.

My Self-Investment (MSI) Savings—a spending plan category, following the pay-yourself-first philosophy, which provides for personal development, retirement, and emergency expenditures.

National Credit Union Administration (NCUA)—a federal agency that monitors and regulates the majority of credit unions, as well as insures money deposited in these credit unions for up to $250,000 per depositor.

Net Price Calculator—an online tool used by students to estimate the net cost of attending a given college for one year. The net price is the total cost of attendance (COA) less projected grants and scholarships. The calculations are made based on answers to questions concerning the student's and his or her family's income, assets, family size, and other relevant information.

non-sufficient funds (NSF)—a banking term used for when an accountholder writes a check, or tries to make an ATM card transaction, for more money than is in the account. The bank or credit union may charge the accountholder an NSF fee.

opt in—when an individual gives permission to participate in something, usually some type of financial service. For example, certain banking services will not apply to your bank account unless you opt in for them.

opt out—when an individual prohibits participation in something, like an optional banking service.

outstanding balance—when speaking of debt, it is the amount of money still owed on an obligation. For example, the dollar amount you currently owe on an auto loan or on your credit card account. In terms of bank accounts, it is the amount of money available in an account, such as how much money you have in your checking account.

overdraft—occurs when an accountholder doesn't have enough money in their account to complete a transaction, and the bank or credit union permits the transaction to go through anyway.

overdraft protection—a service offered by banks and credit unions that allows customers to cover an overdraft in their checking account by using another source of funds at the bank or credit union. A common example is to have money in your savings account transferred to your checking account to cover a shortfall.

penalty fees—a credit card accountholder can trigger a penalty fee by taking such actions as making a payment late or exceeding the credit limit on the card. Look in the credit card agreement and disclosures to find the card penalty policies.

periodic expenses — recurring expenses spaced out over time, such as annual membership dues or semi-annual insurance premium payments.

personal identification number (PIN) — a multi-digit number used to verify your identity to an organization where you have an account. It is a security measure to protect against unauthorized account usage.

portfolio — an investment term referring to an investor's collection of investments, often containing such items as mutual funds, stocks, bonds, ETFs and cash. Portfolios are often identified by purpose, such as a retirement savings portfolio or college savings portfolio.

prepaid card — is a type of debit card, not a credit card. Money is loaded onto the card by the cardholder and then used up as purchases are made. Card activity is not normally reported to credit bureaus and therefore wouldn't contribute to a person's credit history.

principal — a credit term referring to the amount of money borrowed.

prospectus — an informational document that mutual funds and exchange-traded funds make available to the public, as required by federal security laws. The document provides information such as the fund's investment strategy, expenses, performance, risks, and managers' qualifications, as well as other important facts.

qualified withdrawals—account withdrawals that meet specific IRS requirements for that type of account. For example, when referring to IRAs there are age requirements and holding periods to be met by accountholders before making withdrawals if IRS penalties are to be avoided and taxation minimized.

quote—an insurance term referring to the estimated premium a client will be charged for insuring something. Auto, renter's, homeowner's, life, and medical insurance are the most common types for which individuals get quotes.

Reserve Officers' Training Corps (ROTC)—an education-based program offered at colleges, for training students to enter a branch of the military as a commissioned officer after graduation.

rate of return—is the percentage increase or decrease over time in the value of a financial asset or group of assets, such as the change in the value of a stock, bond, or mutual fund share as well as any interest or dividends earned.

rebalancing—the buying and selling of investments in a portfolio to maintain a given asset allocation. As the market value of assets fluctuate, the proportions of various asset classes within a portfolio change. The proportion of these asset classes may need to be adjusted (rebalanced) periodically to maintain target percentages.

resume—a document given to a prospective employer by an applicant, detailing the applicant's educational achievements, work history, experience, skills, and other relevant information.

revolving debt—usually an open-ended debt account where the accountholder can borrow money repeatedly as long as the credit limit is not exceeded and payments on the debt are made according to the account agreement. Credit card accounts are one type of revolving debt.

Roth IRA—a type of individual retirement account into which a person can make after-tax contributions of earnings and later make tax-free withdrawals starting at age 59 and ½ if all IRS requirements are met.

S&P 500 index—a broad-based equity index, created by Standard & Poor's, composed of stocks from 500 leading U.S. companies in leading industries. The value of these 500 companies account for the majority of the U.S. stock market value. The changes in the value of the index approximates the collective returns of the U.S. stock market.

sales tax—a state tax paid by consumers on a range of goods and services. The tax is added to the purchase price at the time of sale.

secured—a type of loan or credit card account where something of value is used as security (collateral) for borrowed money, in the event that the borrower fails to make the agreed loan payments. For example, a car is used as collateral for an auto loan, and the lender may take over ownership of the car if the borrower fails to make payments.

security—an investment term referring to a financial asset that represents an ownership position in something that can be bought or sold. Some of the most common types of securities are stocks and bonds.

Social Security—a federal government program that provides retirement benefits mainly for individuals 62 years and older.

Taxes taken from workers' earnings supply the money to fund this program. The amount retirees and their families receive is partly determined by the age at which the person chooses to retire and the amount of money they have paid into the system. Social Security may also provide payouts to some disabled individuals.

spending plan — a means of planning, controlling, and accounting for the money you earn in contrast to the money you spend or save.

Student Aid Report (SAR) — a report created by the Department of Education, based on a student's FAFSA submission. The document provides the student's EFC and a summary of the student's FAFSA data. The report is sent to the student and any of the schools that he or she has indicated on the FAFSA submission.

subsidized student loan — a type of federal student loan that is granted to students based on financial need as determined from the student's FAFSA. The loans do not accumulate interest charges until the borrower graduates from school. The government is "subsidizing" (paying for) the borrower's interest expense while the student is enrolled at least half-time in college.

target-date mutual fund — a mutual fund that is managed with a fixed future target date in mind, the date when investors are assumed to retire. Using shifting asset allocations, the fund's assets are invested more conservatively as the target date approaches. These type of funds are also known as "lifecycle," "age-based," or "asset allocation" funds and are designed for people saving for retirement.

tax-advantaged—a security, fund, or account that can diminish and/or postpone income taxes on assets.

tax deductions—reductions to taxable income that the government allows individuals to make for certain expenditures, such as money given to charities or contributions made to certain types of retirement accounts. Deductions are claimed on a person's income tax return and can reduce taxes owed.

ticker symbols—a unique abbreviation, normally a string of letters, used to identify a security or fund. For example, mutual funds are typically identified with a string of letters that end in "X," like "VTTSX."

title and registration—documents establishing vehicle ownership and identification. They are required when a car is purchased, either new or used. Each state has its own registration requirements and fees. Periodic registration renewal is usually necessary along with a renewal fee.

unsubsidized student loan—a federal student loan where interest is not subsidized (paid) by the government while the student is enrolled in school. The interest begins to accumulate on the loan as soon as the money is disbursed (distributed).

variable-rate loan—a loan that does not have a fixed rate of interest. The interest rate fluctuates up and down based on an interest rate index. The initial offered interest rate on the variable-rate loan is typically lower than on a comparable fixed-rate loan, but over time the interest rate on the variable-rate loan may adjust upward, often ending up higher than what the fixed rate would have been.

vehicle identification number (VIN)—a string of letters and numbers that are used to identify each manufactured vehicle. The VIN can be used to track the recall history of a car, as well as used by law enforcement for locating stolen vehicles

volatility—in investment terms, this refers to the extent of up and down movement in the rate of return of an investment or group of investments over time.

Wilshire 5000 index—an index composed of stocks representing the majority of U.S. companies, and it is considered representative of the movements of the entire U.S. equities market.

withholding—when an employer holds back a portion of an employee's wages and transmits the money to the government as payment for taxes on behalf of the employee.

withholding allowances—they are used to adjust the amount of money that is withheld for income taxes from an employee's wages. The more allowances the employee claims on Form W-4 the less money will be withheld from the individual's paycheck. A new Form W-4 can be filed whenever an employee wishes to change his or her withholding allowances.

work permit—a document certifying that a minor has legal permission to work at a particular job for a specific employer. Many states require work permits for students. School administration offices normally supply the permit form and usually require that it be completed by the prospective employer and signed by a parent. There are some exclusions from work-permit requirements, for instance, volunteer work and unpaid trainee positions.

work-study—federally subsidized part-time campus jobs for college students. If you receive an acceptance letter from a college, the related financial aid offer frequently includes estimated work-study dollars.

zero-percent financing—a loan that requires no interest payments. As long as the loan agreement terms are followed by the consumer, only the repayment of principal is required. Auto dealers sometimes offer these loans to make a car more attractive to a potential buyer.

Acknowledgments

There are many people I would like to thank for their help and support. I am especially grateful to the following individuals:

My husband, Gary, for enthusiastically supporting my project and for his perceptive input.

Our daughters for constantly cheering me on and for their insightful feedback from a youthful perspective on all or parts of this book.

My parents for their patient readings and great suggestions during my many, many revisions.

My dear friend, Yanna, for offering help and encouragement along the way and for dreaming up the idea of this book with me several years ago.

Last of all, to all the energetic, caring, creative, and optimistic young people everywhere, who were my motivation for this book.

Made in the USA
Lexington, KY
16 August 2018